Mike Boyd

~~Oscar R. Endicht~~

Bless you!

Glenn E. Bininger

The Seven Last Words of Christ

The Seven Last Words of Christ

by

Clem E. Bininger

BAKER BOOK HOUSE
Grand Rapids, Michigan

Library of Congress Catalog Card Number: 71-98138

PHOTOLITHOPRINTED BY CUSHING - MALLOY, INC.
ANN ARBOR, MICHIGAN, UNITED STATES OF AMERICA
1969

Contents

1. The Forgiving Spirit 11
2. Hope for the Hopeless 25
3. The Women in His Life 39
4. Mastering Mental Depression 53
5. On Being Really Human 69
6. Secrets of Satisfied Living 85
7. The Safest Deposit of All 99

1

The Forgiving Spirit

THE FIRST WORD

"Father, forgive them; for they know not what they do."
— Luke 23:34

"Let all bitterness, and wrath, and anger, and clamor, and evil speaking be put away from you, with all malice."
— Ephesians 4:31

"He who has not forgiven an enemy has not yet tasted one of the most sublime enjoyments of life." — Johann K. Lavater

"If we could read the secret history of our enemies we should find in each man's life sorrow and suffering enough to disarm all hostility." — Henry Wadsworth Longfellow

"With malice toward none; with charity for all; with firmness in the right, as God gives us to see the right, let us strive on . . . to bind up the nation's wounds . . . to do all which may achieve and cherish a just and lasting peace among ourselves and with all nations."
— Abraham Lincoln
(Second Inaugural, March 4, 1865)

"My heart was heavy, for its trust had been
Abused, its kindness answered with foul wrong;
So turning gloomily from my fellow men,
One summer Sabbath day I strolled among
The green mounds of the village burial-place;
Where, pondering how all human love and hate
Find one sad level; and how, soon or late,
Wronged and wrongdoer, each with meekened face,
And cold hands folded over a still heart,
Pass the green threshold of our common grave,
Whither all footsteps tend, whence none depart,
Awed for myself, and pitying my race,
Our common sorrow, like a mighty wave,
Swept all my pride away, and, trembling, I forgave!"
— John Greenleaf Whittier

The Forgiving Spirit

"Then said Jesus, Father, forgive them; for they know not what they do." – Luke 23:34

In one of Gladstone's early letters to his wife he remarks,

> "I seem hardly to have any daily pressure . . . no strokes from God; no opportunity for pardoning others, for none offends me."

Unfortunately, however, such unruffled good will is rare. Most of us have some one who offends us . . . some one in whose misery we might unconsciously rejoice.

Yet those of us who are Christian know that we dare not seek the forgiveness of God for ourselves until we ourselves have forgiven those who offend us. Listen to Jesus,

> "If ye forgive men their trespasses, your heavenly Father will also forgive you. But if ye forgive not men their trespasses, neither will your Father forgive your trespasses" (Matthew 6:14-15).

Therefore, we pray in the Lord's Prayer,

> "Forgive us our debts, as we forgive our debtors" (Matthew 6:12).

That is to pray,

> "Our Father in heaven, we only ask that you forgive our trespasses in proportion as we forgive those who trespass against us."

What a dangerous prayer for us all! How can we pray it so glibly?

Or, we dare not expect to worship God effectively so long as anyone holds anything against us. It is not enough passively to forgive; we must actively see to it that our enemies are reconciled to us unless they, too, through hatred for us, bar themselves from communion with God. Listen to Jesus, insisting that mere passive forgiveness grudgingly granted by remote control is not enough:

> "If thou bring thy gift to the altar, and there rememberest that thy brother hath aught against thee . . . [He does not say 'remember that you have anything against thy brother'; if that were all, forgiveness would be comparatively easy – but, if thou there rememberest that thy brother has AUGHT AGAINST THEE,] Leave there thy gift before the altar . . . first, be reconciled to thy brother, and then come and offer thy gift" (Matthew 5:23-24).

Passive forgiveness is not enough! Before we are worthy to worship we must go out of our way again and again to enable our brother to forgive us!

Suffice it to say that you and I have no spiritual life worthy of the name unless we cultivate the forgiving spirit. We may go to church regularly and observe all the forms of religion, but if we are vindictive and bitter – if we carry a chip on our shoulders and everlastingly insist upon what we call our rights" — we deceive ourselves as to our Christianity and the truth is not in us. To paraphrase Paul,

> "Anyone who does not have the Spirit of Christ does not belong to him" (Romans 8:9b).

Small wonder, then, that Jesus' first sentence from the cross is at once so famous and so fascinating. *It is Christianity in miniature!* See the diamond against its dark background of cruelty.

> "When they came to the place which is called The Skull, there they crucified him, and the criminals, one on the right and one on the left" (Luke 23:33).

Never was any man in history more unjustly smitten. The world He loved drove nails into His hands and feet. But the only comment of Jesus upon this outrageous cruelty was,

> "Father, forgive them; for they know not what they do" (Luke 23:34).

Therefore, in a world where revenge is routine and forgivers are few, let's think together about "The Cross and the Forgiving Spirit." There can be no real worship, no real prayer, no real Christianity without that!

I. In the first place, these words of our text are *an eternal reminder that it matters terrifically what you and I believe about God.* To be sure, in many minds theology is taboo and folks say,

> "It doesn't matter what a man believes so long as he lives right."

Moreover, we all understand what our modern minimizers of belief are driving at. They mean that actions speak louder than creeds and that we don't care what church a man goes to if only he does justly, loves mercy, and walks humbly with his God (Micah 6:8). But, for all our sympathetic understanding of those who minimize the older emphasis on creed and dogma, *It still matters terrifically what you and I really believe about God!*

For one thing, it is psychologically impossible to be consistently friendly and forgiving in a universe we believe to be basically unfriendly and unforgiving. Therefore, if Jesus had been an atheist or an agnostic, uncertain of His God, He would never have been able to rise to such divine heights of forgiveness. Too long have we overlooked His preface in the first "Word from the Cross." Listen to it:

> "*Father* [said Jesus] [*Father* . . . Father], forgive them; for they know not what they do" (Luke 23:34).

You see, Jesus, from first to last, and in spite of the difficulties involved in such a faith, *knew that the heart of the universe was presided over by a friendly God!* God was the Father! Men might deny their true nature and be unbrotherly, but God was the Father. What a difference that made in His ability to forgive! *Jesus' belief in the fatherhood of God was the sustaining root out of which the fruit of forgiveness grew!* Of course, it matters what you and I believe!

1. For example, many of us find it hard to forgive because we have become *cynical.* That is to say, we have let "life's buffets and scorns" make us cynical believers in a world of accident and chance. James Stalker puts it beautifully,

> "When righteousness is trampled under foot and wrong is triumphant, faith is always tempted to ask if there really is a God, loving and wise, seated on the throne of the universe, or whether, on the contrary, all is the play of chance. When prosperity is turned suddenly into adversity and the structure of the plans and hopes of a life is tumbled in confusion to the ground, even the child of God is apt to kick against the Divine will.

> Great saints have been driven, by the pressure of pain and disappointment, to challenge God's righteousness in words which it is not lawful for a man to utter. But, when the fortunes of Jesus were at the blackest, when He was baited by a raging pack of wolf-like enemies, and when He was sinking into the unplumbed abysses of pain and desertion, He still said, 'Father' " – (*The Trial and Death of Jesus Christ.* Richard R. Smith, Inc. N.Y. 1930, pp. 189 ff.).

My friends, we can never understand the Master's outer forgiveness without His inner faith. *He refused the sullen cynicism of unbelief.* Even on the Cross He clung tenaciously to the Fatherhood of God. Of course, it matters what you and I believe!

How superficial we are when we look at a man's deed and think of it as independent of his creed! To be sure, it may be independent of his formal creed or denomination, but his real belief is reflected in his conduct every time!

For example, we look at Joseph's forgiveness of his treacherous brothers who had sold him into slavery in Egypt and who, in the end, when Joseph had risen to be Prime Minister, had to stand before him in time of famine to beg bread. We call Joseph "the most Christlike man in the Old Testament" because of his ability to forgive and forget, and we are tempted to cry out,

> "What a forgiving spirit! We don't care what a man believes if only he has a forgiving spirit like Joseph's."

But, listen: according to Joseph himself it was only his great faith in the Fatherly purpose of God which enabled him so to forgive his brothers' treachery. Listen to him,

> "I am Joseph your brother, whom ye sold into Egypt. Now therefore be not grieved, nor angry with yourselves, that ye sold me hither: for God did send me

> before you to preserve life . . . so it was not you that sent me hither but God" (Genesis 45:4 ff.).
> "You meant it unto me for evil, but God meant it for good" (Genesis 50:20a).

To be sure, it goes without saying that it is desperately difficult to see the hand of God in the meanness of our enemies. Such faith and insight, however, are basic and indispensable to the forgiving spirit. In imagination we think of Oxford Square that day in the sixteenth century when they led Hugh Latimer out to burn him at the stake for his Christian faith! Across the centuries we hear again the brave words he spoke to Ridley, his companion in martyrdom:

> "Be of good comfort, Master Ridley, and play the man; we shall this day light such a candle by God's grace in England as, I trust, shall never be put out."

As the flames licked up around his pain-wracked body, Latimer prayed, like his Master, for those who slew him. Ah, but he was able to do that only because of his faith that God is a gracious Father with some good plan behind every life. In the long run *God makes the wrath of wicked men to praise him.* God did use the burned bodies of Latimer and Ridley as a spark which lighted the lamps of religious freedom all over the world!

2. Sometimes we think that we Americans make such a sorry job of our Christianity because of our *tempermental impatience.* We can build skyscrapers successfully but we destroy our dispositions because *we have not the patient faith to wait on God's larger plan.* We want revenge when we want it. Injustice, therefore, quickly goads us to usurp the throne of God. We are not willing to forgive a wrong and leave its redress to a just Father in heaven. Actually, we never think of revenge (the opposite of the forgiving spirit)

in terms of an impatient lack of faith in God's ultimate justice. We, therefore, ignore Paul's admonition which says,

> "Repay no one evil for evil. . . . Beloved, never avenge yourselves, but leave it to the wrath of God; for it is written, 'Vengeance is mine, I will repay, says the Lord'" (Romans 12:17 ff.).

Alas, few of us can be content to commit our enemies patiently to God. We want to usurp the throne of God and exact our own idea of justice. God's justice seems too slow! We really do not believe in the Fatherly justice of God.

Listen, on the other hand, to Peter's interpretation of the secret of Christ's forgiving spirit:

> "Christ . . . suffered for you, leaving you an example, that you should follow in his steps. . . . When he was reviled, he did not revile in return; when he suffered, he did not threaten" (I Peter 2:21 ff.).

But why was He so patiently forgiving? Because, concludes Peter,

> ". . . He trusted to him [God] who judged justly" (I Peter 2:23b).
> "Father, forgive them. . . ." (He said, "Father")

This was His secret — this was the victory which overcame a world of bitterness, even His faith in the Fatherly justice of God. Of course, it matters what you and I believe!

II. Once more, in the second place, these words of our text not only emphasize the importance of belief, but *they are also a striking example of the little-recognized power of the forgiving spirit.* Too long have we regarded forgiveness as an effeminate virtue of the wishy-washy and weak. As a result, we constantly crusade with the sword instead of the Cross! We just do not realize the tremendous power of forgiveness. This, of course, is an old story. Listen to Paul:

> ". . . we preach Christ crucified, a stumbling-block to Jews and folly to Gentiles, but to those who are called, both Jews and Greeks, Christ is the power of God and the wisdom of God. For the foolishness of God is wiser than men, and the weakness of God is stronger than men. . . . God chose what is foolish in the world to to shame the strong" (I Corinthians 1:23 ff.).

And yet, my friends, while we reject the prayer of Christ on the Cross as too slow and too soft, its loveliness haunts us. In our saner moments we know that as Jesus said,

> ". . . all who take the sword will perish by the sword" (Matthew 26:52b).

We know that there is no lasting progress ever made without love that cares enough and dares enough to suffer – love that is brave enough to seem slow and soft – love that is not afraid to lay itself down in mercy to redeem. And *forgiveness does redeem.* Even before the crucifixion was over, one of the two thieves crucified along with Jesus, who at first took part in reviling Him, was converted! The centurion who superintended the execution confessed Him as the Son of God; and, after all was over, multitudes who had been stabbed awake by His forgiving spirit went away beating their breasts! Yes, we preach Christ crucified and forgiving – and the Crucifixion scene itself proves that "the foolishness of God is wiser than men!"

How little we recognize the power of forgiveness!

1. For one thing, we overlook the tremendous lifting power of *self-control.* And *self-control is a major part of forgiveness!* For example, Aaron and Miriam stirred up the children of Israel against the leadership of Moses, and Mo-

ses managed to forgive them not because he was weak but because he was strong! Of his self-control it is written:

> "Now the man Moses was meek, above all the men who were upon the face of the earth" (Numbers 12:3).

But, someone says, the dictionary defines "meek" as "one who is easily cowed." To which we reply that *we have degraded our English word "meek."* In the Greek Old Testament (the Septuagint) and in the Greek of the New Testament the word is *praeis* and *it means self-control!* In the classic Greek wild horses whose powers are domesticated for service are called "meek" – meaning *disciplined and controlled.* In the classic Greek kings who use their great powers constructively are called "meek." Moses, whom Michaelangelo rightly pictures as a powerful giant, is called "meek." And Jesus Himself, the paragon of power brought under control for service, is the "meek and lowly Master, giving rest unto our souls." *Yes, we have degraded our English word "meek."* Let's lift it up again as the Bible does.

> "Blessed [happy] . . . are the meek, for they shall inherit the earth" (Matthew 5:5).

They alone have faith and self-control enough to pray,

> "Father, forgive them; for they know not what they do" (Luke 23:34).

2. Moreover, not only have we misunderstood the power of self-controlled forgiveness to redeem, *we have also missed the power of forgiveness to rebuke and chasten.* Yet what is greater torture to us than to be treated kindly by one whom we have deeply wronged!

> "Therefore [says Paul], if your enemy is hungry, feed him; if he is thirsty, give him drink; for by so doing you

> will heap burning coals upon his head" (Romans 12: 20).

To be sure, a real Christian does not forgive in order to torture people by "burning them up" with kindness; but the fact remains that we cannot return good for evil without heaping coals of fire upon our enemy's head!

During World War I Bishop Jones of the Episcopal Church was deposed by the House of Bishops for his conscientious objection to war as a means of settling anything permanently. During the war he was despised and rejected of men, a man of sorrows and acquainted with grief. Yet in the isolated post to which he was "exiled" for the duration he "did not strive or cry, neither was his voice lifted in the streets." Some years after World War I, the House of Bishops finally reached Bishop Jones' wartime position and plainly said so in their pronouncements against the war method. Naturally, they all had Bishop Jones on their collective conscience. They could not forget how he had forgiven them when they had "transferred him to exile in an obscure post." Day and night they lived with inner voices which cried,

> "What are you going to do about Bishop Jones?"
> "What are you going to do about Bishop Jones?"

Finally they could stand it no longer. They reinstated him with apologies!

> "The weakness of God is stronger than men" (I Corinthians 1:25b).

Bishop Jones, with disciplined forgiveness, had unconsciously heaped coals of fire upon their heads!

3. But perhaps even more potent than the power of forgiveness to redeem or rebuke, is *the power of a forgiving*

spirit to strengthen the forgiver himself. By praying for His enemies, Jesus was enabled to drive back the spirits of anger and revenge which tried to force their poison into His soul. As it is written in the Bible proverb,

> "The merciful man doeth good to his own soul: but he that is cruel troubleth his own flesh" (Proverbs 11:17).

Or, as the proverb reads, which Paul only quoted partly in his letter to the Romans,

> "If thine enemy be hungry, give him bread to eat; and if he be thirsty, give him water to drink: For thou shalt heap coals of fire upon his head, *and the Lord shall reward thee*" (Proverbs 25:21, 22).

Friends, I don't know why Paul omitted that last phrase:

> "Forgive [says the Old Testament proverb] *and the Lord shall reward thee.*"

It is always so. As Jesus summed it up in His Sermon on the Mount,

> "Blessed are the merciful, for they shall obtain mercy . . ." (Matthew 5:7).

Mercy from man and from God is the reward of the merciful and forgiving!

Therefore, we are not ashamed of the gospel of Christ, for it is *the power of God unto salvation!* Forgiveness is not weak. When it is rooted in faith in God and flowers in self-control, it redeems, rebukes, and empowers. Forgiveness, like mercy,

> ". . . is twice blessed
> It blesseth him that gives, and him that takes:

(Weak, ah no!")

> 'Tis mightiest in the mightiest: it becomes
> The throned monarch better than his crown . . .
>
> It is an attribute of God himself,
> An earthly power doth then show likest God's,
> When mercy seasons justice. Therefore . . .
> Though justice be thy plea, consider this,
>
> That in the course of justice none of us
> Should see salvation. We do pray for mercy
> And that same prayer doth teach us all to render
> The deeds of mercy. ("The Merchant of Venice," William Shakespeare)
>
> "Forgive us our debts, O God, as we forgive those who trespass against us!" (Matthew 6:12).

O Lord our God, long-suffering and full of compassion; be present with us, we beseech Thee, as we come before Thee with our sorrows and our sins, to ask for comfort and forgiveness. We thank Thee for meditation and prayer in which we recall our Saviour's sufferings and celebrate His triumph over hatred, bitterness, resentment and death.

Grant us the aid of Thy Holy Spirit, that as we acknowledge our deep need to be forgiven and to forgive, we may be enabled to find peace with Thee and to live peaceably with all men – even our enemies and foes – through Jesus Christ our Lord. Amen

2

Hope for the Hopeless

THE SECOND WORD

"Verily, I say unto you, today you will be with me in paradise." — Luke 23:43

"That day which you fear as being the end of all things is the birthday of your eternity." — Seneca

"When I go down to the grave I can say, like many others, 'I have finished my day's work!' But I cannot say, 'I have finished my life.' My day's work will begin again the next morning. The tomb is not a blind alley; it is a thoroughfare. It closes on the twilight, it opens on the dawn."

— Victor Hugo

"When you take the wires of the cage apart, you do not hurt the bird, but you help it. You let it out of its prison. How do you know that death does not help me when it takes the wires of my cage down? — that it does not release me, and put me into some better place and better condition of life?" — Bishop Randolph S. Foster

"There is no death! What seems so is a transition."

— Henry Wadsworth Longfellow

"Life is a voyage that's homeward bound."

— Herman Melville

Hope for the Hopeless

"Today, shalt thou be with me in paradise."

— Luke 23:43b

As soon as one tries to interpret the Scripture passage which contains our text, he is startled by the difficulty of knowing just where to begin. For the whole incident of the penitent thief and of the subsequent *second sentence of Jesus from the Cross* is rightly called a compendium of theology or "the gospel in miniature." Indeed, there is scarcely a Christian doctrine upon which it does not shed some suggestive light.

1. For example, one might regard this passage as *the only example of death-bed* (or last minute) *repentance in the Scriptures.* Moreover, some have even gone so far as to use the thief's last minute salvation as an excuse for their neglect of the church. There is the old story about the stingy soul who said to the minister,

> "Why should I lead a good life? The thief on the cross got into paradise without it. Why should I unite with a church? The thief on the cross never belonged to a

> church. The thief on the cross never made a pledge to a church budget or otherwise contributed a cent."

And the minister rightly replied,

> "The only difference between you and the dying thief is that *you are a* living *thief.*"

At any rate, while this incident teaches us not to despise death-bed repentance, it certainly does not encourage us to wait until the last minute to set our spiritual house in order. *The other thief is a solemn warning.* Though on the threshold of death and so close to the inspiring presence of Christ, the other thief was only hardened and made more reckless than ever. He went into eternity with blasphemy on his lips! This passage, then, insists that *now is the time to repent!* For

> "We cannot kindle when we will
> The fire that in the soul resides:
> The Spirit breatheth and is still. . . .
> In mystery the soul abides."

2. Again, one might regard this passage about Jesus and the thief as *a striking example of sudden conversion.* According to the story in the other two Gospels (Matthew and Mark) this thief blasphemed with his profane companion one moment and bowed in penitent prayer the next! Moreover, the desire to explain away the suddenness of the conversion has led to great speculation as to previous meetings between the thief and Christ. To be sure, the thief had heard Jesus pray for the forgiveness of His enemies in His first sentence on the Cross. The jeers of Jesus' enemies informed him that Christ claimed to be Divine. More than likely the thief was in the courtroom to witness and hear our Lord's trial before Pilate. But when we try to go back beyond that, we have nothing but pure supposition.

Had he ever heard Jesus preach? Had he witnessed any of His miracles? How much did the thief know of the Kingdom when he prayed,

> "Lord, remember me, when thou comest into thy kingdom!" (Luke 23:42).

We may guess at the answers to these questions, but the record does not say. I should be inclined, like James Stalker, to look even further back. *The thief may have come from a religious home!* He may have been a prodigal son led astray by bad company – especially by the blasphemous companion with whom he is now being crucified for murder. Therefore, just as there was a weeping mother at the foot of the Cross of Jesus, there may have been a heartbroken mother at the foot of the other cross also – the thief's mother whose patient prayers were about to be answered beyond her fondest dreams. More things are wrought by a mother's prayers than this world dreams of!

Suffice it to say that the possibility of sudden conversion is usually argued with more heat than light by both sides. Suppose, for example, someone reading these words – someone knowing that he is not now consciously, willfully, and happily a child of God – suppose you should turn to God completely in this very moment. Would that be sudden conversion? Yes, but the preparation for it has been going on for years. There are the religious teachings you have received from childhood, the prayers offered in your behalf, the Christian personalities who have wooed you out of yourself, the secret strivings of the Spirit of God for your spirit – all these influences have but led up to this sudden change. Though your conversion were to take place this very instant, it would only be the last step in a process which has gone on for years!

Yet in a sense it would be sudden. And why should it not? What real reason is there why your complete return to God should be further postponed? It has been well said concerning the wooing of God's transforming Spirit,

> " 'Tis seldom offered twice; seize, then, the hour
> When conscience speaks, and duty points the way."

3. Or, yet again, one might regard this passage as *a most unique testimony to the deity of Christ.* Here a poor, dying wretch, without previous prejudice, sees Jesus despised and rejected of men, yet dares to pray to our Lord as a God! Strange, isn't it? But stranger still is the startling fact that Jesus, who is always so frank and honest and humble, did not say,

> "Don't pray to me; I am a mere man like yourself, and I know as little of the unknown world into which we are both going as you do."

That is what Jesus should have answered if He is a mere man as so many make Him out to be. But, no, *he accepted the prayer of the penitent!* He spoke of the world unseen as His familiar native land! He let the thief believe that He possessed as much influence in Heaven as He was credited with. My friends, if Jesus be not more than mortal man, He is an egotistical fanatic who took advantage of the credulity of a suffering soul! He was prayed to as a God and He accepted the prayer, saying,

> "Today, shalt thou be with me in paradise" (Luke 23:43b).

4. Or, we might interpret our text as *a miniature snapshot of the future life.* It definitely denies purgatory, that half-way house, where sinful souls are supposed to "sweat out their own salvation in fear and cleansing."

> "*Today* [immediately, says Jesus — *today*], shalt thou be with me in paradise" (Luke 23:43b).

Again, it denies the late Judge Rutherford's doctrine of "soul sleep" – the teaching that departed spirits sleep until the last judgment. Instead our text insists upon *a conscious, intermediate state where Christ is and where we know each other,* while waiting for our new resurrection bodies (adequate vehicles for the soul) in which we will be finally judged. Notice, the personal pronouns, hinting at once of both consciousness and identity:

> "Today, shalt *thou* be with *me* in paradise" (Luke 23: 43b).

As Paul puts it,

> "To be absent from the body is to be at home with the Lord" (II Corinthians 5:8).

Of course, for the wicked the presence of Christ either here or hereafter is hellish; for the penitent only is Christ's presence paradise – both here and hereafter!

5. Still again, one might use this incident as an example of Paul's summary of *what it means to be a Christian.* Christianity, says Paul, is

> ". . . repentance toward God and faith in the Lord Jesus Christ" (Acts 20:21).

To be sure, repentance and faith may involve many and complex things but we see them both in the thief's words. His "repentance toward God" is brought out by what he said to rebuke his profane companion,

> "Dost thou not fear God?" (Luke 23:40).

His faith in Christ as Lord is sublimely expressed in his prayer,

> "*Lord* [under the cruel and humiliating circumstances

> — think of calling the crucified, Lord], remember me, when thou comest into thy kingdom" (Luke 23:42).

In Luther's beautiful comment:

> "God could not allow His Son ever to be completely destitute of subjects, and now His church survived for the instant only in this one man. Where the faith of St. Peter broke off, the faith of the penitent thief began."

6. Or, once more we might stress the striking fact that *this incident is but a typical cross section of the life of Christ.* Long before they had derided Him as

> "a friend of publicans and sinners" (Matthew 11:19).

Now, by crucifying Him between two thieves, they unconsciously put the same idea into action. As our Lord Himself said,

> "The Son of man is come to seek and to save that which is lost" (Luke 19:10).

He had lived among sinners; it was altogether fitting and proper that He should die in their midst!

My friends, Jesus is always in the midst of sinners. He is even now in our midst. And the strange behavior of the two thieves on the neighboring crosses is typical of what happens every day: *Some sinners believe and find peace, while others do not!* Thus it shall be until the end of time — and on the Day of Judgment when the whole history of the world is wound up Jesus will still be in the midst — with *the penitent on one side and the impenitent on the other!* It is an awesome picture, but it is true to experience. He comes unto His own offering abundant life — offering peace and power, but too often we receive Him not; but

> "as many as received him, to them gave he power to become the sons of God" (John 1:12).

The cross and a dying thief! Surely, this is a compendium of theology and a "miniature of the gospel": death-bed repentance, sudden conversion, the Deity of Christ, the future life, repentance and faith, the unpardonable sin of finally rejecting Christ – all these chapters on theology are here in miniature! For a few minuntes more, however, let us look at this scene again to see if there is something more to remember.

I. In the first place, looked at from the point of view of Jesus Himself, this familiar passage is *a word of challenge to the afflicted.* It insists that God never completely lets us down. We need never feel completely useless. No situation is ever so cruel and dark as to be without its possibilities for helping someone else. Even on the Cross *Christ was given a hopeless thief to comfort and forgive.* In Burleigh's significant sentence,

> "There never was a day that did not bring its own opportunity for doing good, . . . good that could never have been done before, and can never be done again."

What a challenge to us, who, in our afflictions, are prone to grumble and complain! What if we, like the Master, even on the Cross, were sensitive to the need of somebody close at hand!

No trouble is ever given us that a Christ-like spirit cannot transform into an opportunity for service. A few years after the crucifixion Paul and Silas, two early Christians, are unjustly imprisoned; their feet are in stocks and their backs are bleeding from the Roman lash, but they are by no means useless. No, their cheery songs in the night so impress their callous Philippian jailer that, after the earthquake, he thinks of God in terms of His servants, Paul and Silas, and falls at their feet to pray,

> "What must I do to be saved?" (Philippians 16:30).

And, Paul and Silas, forgetting their peeves and their pains, give eternal answer,

> "Believe on the Lord Jesus Christ and thou shalt be saved, and thy household" (Acts 16:31).

God never lets us down completely. In our darkest hours, if only our souls are sensitive, God always gives us some Philippian jailer or some dying thief to serve. As someone has said,

> "Even disorder and pain, when rightly interpreted, may be regarded as ghosts that prowl in the basement of your nature to drive you to a higher level of service."

At any rate, Jesus' concern for the thief on the cross is *a challenge to the afflicted.* God never lets us down completely. Some one in special need is always provided for you and me to serve – in sickness or in health – as long as we each shall live!

II. In the second place, looked at from the point of view, not of Jesus, but of the thief, these words are *a message of hope for the hopeless.* For, alas, we do not all have the Christian grace to see our crosses with the eyes of Christ. What if our past training is so shallow and our past moral life so shabby that we have no reserve of spiritual power when our troubles come? It is one thing to talk about the redemptive element in imitating the helpful patience of Jesus, but we must never forget that all His life Jesus had habitually gone about being patient and good. Our Lord's power on Calvary's cross was but the last link in a cable of habit into which He had woven a sacrificial thread each day until at last on the Cross it had become so strong He could not break it! But, alas, the dying thief was not fortified with the habit of loving service. He had no impetus from a good past and no more time for a good future. Surely, then, someone says,

> "Salvation has to be more than a mere patient gritting of one's teeth or a blissful brightening of the corner where you are."

To which we answer,

> "It is here that we come to the heart of the gospel. *What hope is there for sinners who stand naked and shivering on the brink of eternity?*"

If someone says,

> "That is an old fashioned fundamentalist question."

We say,

> "Yes, but it is a question we ministers see unspoken on the lips of every family which, puzzled and dejected, buries its black sheep in premature death."

What about the loved one who reaches the end of his days with no good past to recount and no more future to redeem? That question may be old-fashioned but it is persistent!

In Dr. Stalker's striking statement,

> "There is no more critical test of theologies and theologians than the question of what message we have for a dying person whose sins are unforgiven. If the salvation the preacher has to offer is only a course of moral improvement, what can he have to say to one who has no more time to improve?" – (*The Trial and Death of Jesus Christ*. Op. cit., p. 207).

To be sure, we usually take comfort from the fact that we never know whether or not God's redeeming Spirit penetrates an ebbing life even into the depths of coma. Moreover, on the basis of Christian standards no one of us ever merits salvation. As Paul says,

> "We all have sinned and come short of the glory of God" (Romans 3:23).

Therefore, we must all put our ultimate trust in the mercy of God in Christ. Furthermore, we rest assured that no matter how much we may love someone, God loves him even more. Yet, if we are serious-minded people, we are never comfortable about our loved ones until some repentance is obvious and evident, like the thief's who cried,

> "Lord, remember me, when thou comest into thy Kingdom" (Luke 23:42).

and heard the blessed assurance,

> "Today, shalt thou be with me in paradise" (Luke 23:43b).

This is the good news of the gospel. No matter how belated, there is hope for the hopeless if only he will turn as the thief did to Christ! As Isaiah insisted,

> "Though your sins be as scarlet, they shall be white as snow" (Isaiah 1:18).

Forgiveness immediate, joyful, and complete! As much as this good news can be abused and cheapened by fire-eating revivalists, there is no gospel without this *hope for the hopeless!* In Christ there is forgiveness, immediate, joyful, and complete!

Moreover, do not think that hopelessness is confined to dying sinners. Alas, how many of us feel hopeless at this very moment! Often we feel inferior, inadequate for life, useless misfits to whom theology and psychology are not very convincing. To be sure, our modern psychology about saving ourselves in the service of others is a needed emphasis and we have already made it in this very message. But, friends, there are times when we cannot help others much until we ourselves are helped from on High.

Martin Luther, for example, as a Roman Catholic monk, tried to save himself by good works alone. Like any good Boy Scout or Service Club enthusiast Luther went about doing good. He knew that faith without works is dead. But for all his fasting, for all his slaving and tense toiling to be acceptable to God, for all his sincere attempts to struggle and strain his way into God's favor, Luther failed. Somehow the blessed assurance – the peace and power of it – eluded his tense and troubled soul. Then his spiritual advisor, a wise old monk named John Staupitz, said in effect,

> "Martin, you are trying to save yourself by good works. Instead of accepting God's mercy by faith, you are trying to buy off the Divine wrath with service. Remember, in our creed it is also written, 'I believe in the forgiveness of sins.'"

Ah, my soul, how we wish someone reading this – someone troubled about his past, nervous about his present, and anxious about his future – how we wish someone who feels hopeless could catch this "*Let go – Let God*" aspect of our Christian faith! In a day when psychiatrists' offices and ministers' studies are filled with victims of our American activism, it is not enough to tell these frayed out and hopeless souls to "be brave and love each other." They need – we all need – a vision of the eternal God and an experience of His power to lift – not only the wise and good – but also the foolish and weak!

> "Today, thou shalt be with me in paradise" (Luke 23: 43b).

The wonder of it! These words came not to a paragon of virtue, joyous in the service of his fellow men. They came to a dying thief – a message of *hope to the hopeless!* Say it to yourself this very moment,

> "I believe in the forgiveness of sins."
> "Lord, remember me when thou comest into thy kingdom" (Luke 23:42).

Almighty God, spirit of peace and of grace, whose salvation is never far from penitent hearts; we confess the sins that have estranged us from Thee, dimmed our vision of heavenly things, and brought upon us many troubles and sorrows. We remember with shame how often we have forgotten our duties and lost our faith.

O merciful Father, grant unto us who humble ourselves before Thee, the remission of all our sins and the assurance of Thy pardon and peace; through Him who has indeed come unto His kingdom with transforming power. Amen

3

The Women in His Life

THE THIRD WORD

"Woman, behold thy son! . . . Behold, thy mother!"
— John 19:26, 27

"At the end only two things really matter to a man, regardless of who he is, and they are the affection and understanding of his family. . . . The family is an everlasting anchorage, a quiet harbor where a man's ships can be left to swing in the moorings of pride and loyalty." — Admiral Richard E. Bird, *Alone*

"For God's sake look after our people." — Captain Scott (Freezing to death in the Antarctic)

"History teaches us that there is no substitute for the family if we are to have a society that stands for human beings at their best." — Ray Lyman Wilbur

"Lord, behold our family here assembled. We thank Thee for this place in which we dwell; for the love that unites us; for the peace accorded us this day; for the hope with which we expect the morrow, for the health, the work, the food, and the bright skies that make our lives delightful, for our friends in all parts of the earth, and our friendly helpers in this foreign isle." — Robert Louis Stevenson

"The family is the nucleus of civilization." — Will Durant

"The domestic affections are the principal source of human happiness and well-being." — Charles W. Eliot

"The ideal which the wife and mother makes for herself, the manner in which she understands duty and life, contain the fate of the community. . . . Woman is the salvation or destruction of the family. She carries its destinies in the fold of her mantle." — Henri F. Amiel

The Women in His Life

". . . and certain women, who had been healed of evil spirits and infirmities, Mary called Magdalene, out of whom went seven devils; and Joanna, the wife of Chuza, Herod's treasurer, and Susanna, and many others, who ministered unto Him of their substance." – Luke 8:2, 3

"Now there stood by the cross of Jesus, his mother; and his mother's sister [Salome]; Mary, the wife of Cleophas; and Mary Magdalene." – John 19:25

"Son, behold thy mother. . . ." – John 19:27

To many people it is a little known fact that, during His days of popularity, our Lord was followed day by day not only by twelve male disciples, but by *a host of adoring women.* These ladies not only forsook the comforts of home and followed Him all the way from Galilee; they also willingly and gladly paid His expenses and otherwise looked after His personal comfort! This is the plain meaning of the words which occur several times in the New Testament:

". . . and the twelve were with him, and *certain women*

> . . . *who ministered* unto him of their substance" (Luke 8:3)

Indeed, four of these women followed Him even after His death by crucifixion, for Luke tells us that

> ". . . the women also, who came with him from Galilee, followed after, and beheld the sepulchre, and how his body was laid. And they returned and prepared spices and ointments . . ." (Luke 23:55, 56a).

One of these faithful women, Mary Magdalene, was the first to reach the empty tomb on the first Easter morning, so that it can be truly said that

> "Women were the last to leave the Cross and a woman was the first to visit the Empty Tomb, and the latter, *Mary Magdalene,* taking the good news to the disciples, *became the first preacher of the Resurrection.*"

I. Consider, then, that *we have in the ministry of these adoring women an amazing testimony to the revolutionary message and high character of Jesus.*

1. For one thing, we have here *the beginnings of the long struggle for the emancipation of women!* In the time of Christ – and in the Orient – women were regarded as inferior to men. They were thought to be fit only for domestic service and maternal ministries. As a matter of fact, in those distant days, few people of either sex were willing to brave the dangers or endure the trials of primitive travel. To find, therefore, women of position and wealth who would risk both their reputations and their lives to live like gypsies, was downright amazing! That a Rabbi or Teacher like Jesus would be so unconventional as to enlist women disciples was radical and revolutionary! Here, then, we have *the beginnings of the long struggle for the emancipation of women.* And because of this radical

teaching of Jesus concerning the spiritual equality of the sexes Paul later dared to write for all to read,

> ". . . there is neither Gentile nor Jew, . . . bond nor free: but *Christ is* all, and *in all* [including women]" (Colossians 3:11).

2. Again, we have in these ministering women *a powerful testimony to the moral integrity and sinless perfection of the Master!*" Think for a moment of the malicious and bitter enemies of Jesus. How craftily and constantly they watched His every move that they might have something with which to accuse Him! Yet His fellowship with these women was on such a lofty plane that His enemies dared not even bribe false witnesses to breathe a breath of scandal! In the end Jesus' enemies had to trump up vague charges about His being a revolutionist who was not Caesar's friend. This fact, that nobody ever accused Jesus of improper conduct with these women in His retinue, is the more striking when we remember that in those days only loose women ventured away from their homes; and, of course, no respectable Teacher or Rabbi even dared to be seen talking in public to a woman of any kind: good, bad, or indifferent! Yes, in the complete absence of scandal, real or imagined, we have here *a potent testimony to the moral integrity and sinless perfection of the Master!*

II. In the second place, however, in the ministry of these women we have not only the Master's revolutionary message about the spiritual equality of the sexes and a potent testimony to His moral integrity; *we also see how easy it is for us to desert our Lord when trouble comes.*

In other words, we must not over-idealize these women. Not all of them stuck it out until the bitter end. On the contrary, there is evidence that the more socially prominent among them forsook Him when toward the end it became clear that the Roman authorities were about to crucify Him. In Chapter 8 Luke names three women, two of whom were prominent, who made a good start as followers of Jesus. Listen to the story:

> "He went throughout every city and village, preaching and showing the glad tidings of the Kingdom of God . . . and the twelve disciples were with him, and certain women, who had been healed of evil spirits and infirmities" (Luke 8:1, 2).

Then follows the listing by name of three women who had been healed of either mental or physical illness:

> "*Mary called Magdalene,* out of whom went seven devils, and *Joanna* the wife of Chuza, Herod's treasurer, and *Susanna* . . ." (Luke 8:3).

Now Luke, you remember, was a Gentile – the only Gentile writer of Holy Scripture. Moreover, he was a professional man – a physician of Philippi, a Roman city. Luke's Gospel, therefore, is slanted to impress Romans, Greeks, and other non-Jews. Therefore, Luke took pardonable pride in listing the important people whose names were on the roll of disciples. In a sense, Mary Magdalene was a "nobody" but, just think of it:

> "Joanna the wife of Chuza, Herod's treasurer, and Susanna . . ." (Luke 8:3)

Joanna was the wife of King Herod's trusted business manager and treasurer. *Susanna* was in the social register of her day. Her name was doubtless on letterheads as a sponsor of good causes, and she was spoken of reverently in the society pages. Yes, Joanna and Susanna were prominent people with important connections! But, alas, where were these influential women at Calvary? Even in Luke's account of the crucifixion, the names of Joanna and Susanna are conspicuous by their absence!

We all know how it is. There are times when it is best not "to stick one's neck out," as the saying goes. So Joanna may have developed a headache and Susanna suddenly had guests from out of town. Maybe husband Chuza, Herod's treasurer, said to Joanna,

> "Joanna, I am putting my foot down. This Jesus is not Herod's friend. Pilate is putting on the pressure. The time has come to choose between Jesus and my job."

What Susanna's spouse said we do not even guess at. But it is clear that only Mary Magdalene, who had no husband to restrain her, was around at Calvary! Yes, it is easy to follow Jesus when there is nothing controversial afoot and the preacher simply shows the

> "glad tidings of the Kingdom of God" (Luke 8:1).

It is easy to get some help from religion for mind and body then, being helped, to forsake the Lord when "glad tidings" become "bad tidings"! However, you and I must not be too hard on Joanna and Susanna. Their husbands may have done just what any self-respecting husband of today would do to keep his wife out of trouble with the law. Moreover, when the Cross came, all the Master's male disciples, except John, forsook Him and fled!

III. In the third place, however, notice that *some of the adoring women stuck it out until the bitter end – and beyond!* John gives us this picture,

> "Now there stood by the cross of Jesus, *his mother;* his mother's sister; Mary the wife of Cleophas; and Mary Magdalene" (John 19:25).

Most scholars are agreed that at least four women, three of them relatives of Jesus, stood by at Calvary. They were:

1. His mother, *Mary of Nazareth;*
2. Her sister, *Salome,* the wife of Zebedee and mother of His favorite cousins, James and John;
3. *Mary Cleopas,* the sister-in-law of Mary of Nazareth and Salome, who was the mother of two other disciples, James the Less and Joseph;
4. And last but not least, *Mary Magdalene!*

Now see the differing motives that give us staying power in life's crises.

1. For one thing, there is *family loyalty and love.* All three mothers, the Virgin Mary, Salome, and Mary Cleopas were being courageously loyal to their sons. Jesus, James and John, James the Less and Joseph (all cousins) were in deep danger and mother love did not desert them. More than likely the beloved disciple, John, who was the rich relative of the High Priest and as such had safely witnessed the trial of Jesus, ran home as soon as the death sentence was passed and told the Master's family of the coming Crucifixion! Immediately the Virgin Mother sent word to her sister, Salome, and doubtless Salome said,

> "Mary, we must tell our brother's wife, Mary Cleopas! After all her boys, James the Less and Joseph, are in this much as our own sons are."

And the three mothers – related by blood and marriage – made their brave journey to the Cross out of maternal love and family loyalty!

Yes, how close the bonds of family are! Salome, the wife of Zebedee and mother of James and John, you remember, was terrifically ambitious for her sturdy sons. She had watched them leave their aged father, Zebedee, and his prosperous fishing fleet to follow their cousin Jesus. Later she tried to regain the loss by slipping up to Jesus and saying,

> "When thou comest into thy glory, bid my sons to sit the one on your right hand and the other on the left" (Matthew 20:21).

History has condemned her for this as a self-centered and ambitious mother; but why not ask her nephew, Jesus, to take care of His favorite cousins? Is not blood thicker than water? Was not the Master's mother, Mary, Salome's very own sister?

At any rate, it is to Salome's eternal credit that, although she was ambitious in comparative prosperity, she was also brave in adversity! She got sister-in-law, Mary Cleophas, and they tried to comfort their kinswoman, Jesus' mother, at the Cross! When Jesus uttered His third sentence from the Cross, saying to His beloved disciple, John,

> "Son, behold your mother; mother behold your [new] son . . ." (John 19:27),

the Master thus turned His widowed mother over to the keeping and care of His cousin, John. It was John's mother, Salome, who became the hospitable mistress of the comfortable Jerusalem home into which her sister, Mary of Nazareth, came!

Several years ago we visited the Bible lands and a high point of our trip was the village of Emmaus. On that first Easter afternoon, the Risen Christ walked the seven mile road from Jerusalem to Emmaus and overtook two heartbroken disciples who did not recognize their Lord in His Risen Body, and they told Him of their sorrow. Finally, reaching Emmaus, they said to their still unknown traveling companion,

> "Stay with us, for it is toward evening and the day is now far spent" (Luke 24:29).

So we walked the road to Emmaus in the late afternoon and took a picture of the clock on the church tower — with the hands at five minutes after six. Inside the church at Emmaus there is a mural showing the two disciples with whom Jesus walked incognito on that first Easter afternoon. Luke tells us that one was named Cleophas and the artist, who made the mural, pictures the other disciple as a woman! How natural that would be! Let your imagination range a bit. Jesus rises from the dead on Easter morning and heads, before the day is done, toward Emmaus, the home of His mother's brother, Cleophas, and His Aunt Mary Cleophas! Not wanting to endanger His mother and His aunt Salome in Jerusalem, He decides instead to spend the afternoon in the country with His mother's brother, Cleophas, and his wife, Mary! Yes, how close the bonds of family are! Three of the four adoring women at the Cross were relatives who together had five sons in the Christian cause!

2. But, my friends, more remarkable than the bonds of family love — and stronger — are *the ties of sheer gratitude for underserved redemption* which made Mary Magdalene stand by the Cross until the bitter end — and beyond! The sorrow of Mary Magdalene was very deep. The Master had delivered her from severe mental illness and now, alas, her Friend and Counsellor seemed forever beyond the reach of her devotion!

We wish we could absolve Mary Magdalene of the popular and terrible misconception concerning her reputation. For some reason, almost without exception, the term "Magdalene" has become a synonym for a fallen woman. Yet there is absolutely no proof in Scripture for this slanderous charge. Mary Magdalene simply means — Mary of Magdala — just as we speak of our Lord's mother as Mary of Nazareth. Magdala was her home town, and the title is used by the Gospel writers simply to distinguish her from the other women who bore the name of Mary.

To be sure, it is true that she had

"— been delivered from seven demons" (Luke 8:2b),

and this phrase was sometimes used by Jewish writers as descriptive of some terrible form of sin, such as drunkenness or impurity, but *it was more often used to describe different forms of mental or nervous disease.* Attempts have been made to link Mary Magdalene with the Bible's "woman who was a sinner" who washed Jesus' feet with her tears, but the case has never been proven; and, in the absence of positive proof, we have no right to link Mary Magdalene's memory with the sin of unchastity and prostitution.

We believe that *the demons possessing her had afflicted her with a mental illness which had recurred seven times from her youth.* At any rate, Mary of Magdala was present at His Cross, watching the cruel crucifixion and the humiliating death of Him who had so sympathetically restored her to sanity and mental health! Her grateful heart was wrung with anguish. Jesus, to Mary Magdalene, was far more than mere blood relative and kin! *He was the Lord of her restored life!*

As Mary, our Lord's mother, was led away from the Cross by Salome and Mary Cleophas and John, Mary Magdalene stayed on as they took His broken body down from the Cross — tearing the flesh in His dead hands and feet in the brutal process. Then Mary of Magdala — and certain unnamed women from Galilee — followed the funeral procession to Joseph of Arimathea's garden where they laid Him in a new tomb. Luke gives us the picture:

> ". . . they followed after, and beheld the sepulchre, and how the body was laid. And they returned, and prepared spices and ointment" (Luke 23:55-56).

Then, being good Jews, they rested the full day on the Saturday sabbath, as required by their ancient faith.

For Mary Magdalene, however, the Sabbath was but a nightmare of heartbreak and tortured dreams. Early Sunday morning, while it was yet dark, she returned to Joseph's lovely garden to mourn. She feared for her sanity, now that her calm Friend and Counsellor seemed forever gone. And, then, in the garden's shadows of early dawn, she saw a ghostly figure. Supposing him to be the gardener, she cried out,

> "Sir, they have taken away my Lord and I know not where they have laid Him" (John 20:13).

And, then, the Risen Lord spoke His very first word after Resurrection. He said (simply)

> "Mary!" (John 20:16a).

And Mary of Magdala, from whom seven devils had gone forever, rushed to His feet and cried,

> "Master . . ." (John 20:16b).

The conclusion of the matter, then, is this. Our ties to Christ this day — as always — are mixed and varied. Some serve in the church because they meet in its fellowship important people — people like Joanna and Susanna! But all too often prestige-seeking Christians fall away when the clouds of opposition appear on the horizon — or when the church has a Building Campaign. Others, like Salome, are ambitious for their children — want them to have choral training, Christian education, spiritual advantage, or a reputation for conventional goodness. Still others, like Mary Cleophas, stand by because they have relatives who are church-minded and who think discipleship is important.

But, friends, those who have real staying power and work everlastingly in the service of Christ in all kinds of weather are those, like Mary Magdalene, who sense their deep personal need which only Christ can meet in this world and the next! The most powerful motivation and the most stubborn staying power belong only to those of us who sense our need and have turned to Christ as our personal Saviour and Friend. The steadfast are invariably the humbly grateful who have known the joy of being called by their first names by Christ on some transforming Easter morning of the soul! These are the thankful who know they can never pay back the debt of love they owe, but who sing with tearful joy,

"Beneath the Cross of Jesus,
I fain would take my stand –
The shadow of a mighty Rock
Within a weary land;
A home within the wilderness,
A rest upon the way,
From burning of the noon-tide heat,
And the burden of the day.

"Upon the Cross of Jesus
Mine eye at times can see
The very dying form of One,
Who suffered there for me:
And from my stricken heart with tears
Two wonders I confess –
The wonders of redeeming love
And my unworthiness.

"I take, O cross, thy shadow
For my abiding place:
I ask no other sunshine than
The sunshine of His face;
Content to let the world go by,
To know no gain nor loss:
My sinful self my only shame,
My glory, all, the cross."

O Thou, who by giving Thy Son to be born of Mary didst sanctify motherhood and exalt the families of earth: bless, we pray Thee, our homes, kindred and friends. Grant that our hearts may be glad and all our pleasures of the family circle pure.

Take into Thy keeping our loved ones from whom we are now separated, and grant that both they and we, by drawing near to Thee, may be drawn closer to one another.

We commend to Thee the poor, the cold, the hungry, the lonely, and those who have no helper. So move the hearts of those to whom Thou hast freely given that we also may freely give through Jesus Christ our Lord. Amen

4

Mastering Mental Depression

THE FOURTH WORD

"My God! My God! Why hast thou forsaken me?"
— Matthew 27:46

"If God be with us, who can be against us?" — Romans 8:31

"Where faith is there is courage, there is fortitude, there is steadfastness and strength. . . . Faith bestows that sublime courage that rises superior to the troubles and disappointments of life, that acknowledges no defeat except as a step to victory; that is strong to endure, patient to wait, and energetic to struggle. . . . Light up, then, the light of faith in your heart. . . . It will lead you safely through the mists of doubt and the black darkness of despair; along the narrow, thorny ways of sickness and sorrow, and over the treacherous places of temptation and uncertainty." — James Allen

"The person who has a firm trust in the Supreme Being is powerful in His power, wise by His wisdom, happy by His happiness." — Joseph Addison

"Abide with me; fast falls the eventide;
The darkness deepens; Lord, with me abide;
When other helpers fail, and comforts flee,
Help of the helpless, O abide with me.

"Swift to its close ebbs out life's little day;
Earth's joys grow dim, its glories pass away;
Change and decay in all around I see;
O Thou who changest not, abide with me.

"Hold Thou Thy cross before my closing eyes;
Shine through the gloom, and point me to the skies;
Heaven's morning breaks, and earth's vain shadows flee;
In life, in death, O Lord, abide with me."

—Henry Francis Lyte

Mastering Mental Depression

"My God, my God, why hast thou forsaken me?"

— Matthew 27:46b

The seven sentences of Christ from the Cross may be divided into two groups. *In the first group* of three, namely, the prayer for His persecutors, the pardon of the penitent thief, and the provision for His widowed mother, *our Lord was so typically dealing with the needs of others. In the second group,* however, of which the text of this message is the first of four, *He is involved with His own deep needs.*

Between these two groups of sayings there elapsed a long period of time. From the sixth hour until the ninth Jesus was silent. And during this interval, from noon until three in the afternoon, there was an eclipse of the sun. It was as if the sun refused to shine on such a deed of inhuman cruelty. During this weird eclipse the sounds around the cross are somewhat muted. But finally the silence is shattered by Christ himself, who, in a loud voice, shouted *the fourth sentence from the Cross,* crying,

"Eli, Eli, lama sabathani?"

That is to say,

> "My God, my God, why hast thou forsaken me? (Matthew 27:46b).

Let it be said at once that this mental depression – this feeling of Jesus that God had "let Him down" – comes to us as a terrific shock. At the Last Supper our Lord had calmly reassured His disciples, saying,

> "Behold, the hour cometh, yea, is now come, that ye shall be scattered every man to his own, and shall leave me alone; and yet I am not alone, because the Father is with me" (John 16:32).

Moreover, we know from history and experience how frequently great saints have died in an ecstasy of communion with God. Martyrs have often been so exhilarated as to sing even as the flames consumed them! Therefore, it is with shocked surprise that we are told that the very opposite of ecstasy and exaltation was in the mind of Jesus. It was mental depression at its blackest,

> "My God, my God, why hast thou forsaken me?" (Matthew 27:46b).

Of course, the deepest question is whether the divine desertion of Jesus was subjective or objective: that is, whether, on account of bodily weakness, He only had a sense of being abandoned, or whether, in any real sense, God had actually forsaken Him and "let Him down."

Well, the crucifixion was a stark revelation of human depravity and degradation. Around the Cross the sin of man reached its epitome and did its awful worst. What was done on Calvary against Christ and against God in Him was an embodiment of the sin of the whole world. And without a doubt it was this close look at sin's utmost cruelty which depressed the sinless Christ. As James Stalker said in effect,

> "He was sickened with sin's contact; He was crushed with its brutality – crushed to death (and by its contamination) separated from God."

Yet He had taken this sinful human nature upon Himself; He was completely identified with our human nature – bone of its bone, flesh of its flesh; and, as in a degenerate family an unusually delicate and refined mother may bear the whole weight and shame of the whole tribe on her frail shoulders, so Jesus felt the unworthiness and seeming hopelessness of our race as if we were His own flesh and blood. Under this intolerable burden of our sinful human nature, voluntarily assumed, the weight became almost unbearable and it seemed that God has "let Him down."

Thus far we may go into the mystery of Christ's mental depression with solid fact beneath our feet. But some theologians have gone farther to say that Jesus was actually forsaken of God. Even Luther and Calvin said that in the hours on the Cross just before this depressed cry our Lord literally "descended into hell" and endured the torments of the damned. And Rambach, a German writer, in his *Meditations on the Sufferings of Christ*, says,

> "God was now dealing with Jesus not as a loving and merciful father with his child, but as an offended and righteous judge with an evildoer. The heavenly Father now regards His Son as the greatest sinner to be found beneath the sun, and discharges on Him the whole weight of His wrath."

Frankly, if you and I should use such extreme language, we would be "over our heads" in morbid speculation not rooted in Scripture. Much to be preferred is the comment of Bengel who says,

"In the fourth word from the Cross our Saviour not only says that He has been delivered into the hands of men, but that He has suffered at the hands of God something unutterable."

And there is here something unutterable. Perhaps the sanest and most vital interpretation of this forbidding feeling of forsakenness on the part of Jesus is rendered in the words of the old hymn first written by a minister's wife to teach little children in one syllable words the doctrine of the atonement,

"There is a green hill far away, without a city wall,
Where the dear Lord was crucified; who died to save us all.

"We may not know, *we cannot tell what pains He had to bear;*
But we believe it was for us, He hung and suffered there.
— Cecil Frances Alexander

So, we do well to avoid speculation. There are many things in the experience of Jesus which are unique and cannot be paralled with our own. Yet there is no doubt — is there — that *you and I are frequently mentally and spiritually depressed. We feel* that God has "let us down." Just when we are safest, suddenly the bottom drops out of everything and we cry in desperation.

"My God, my God, why [why] hast thou forsaken me?" (Matthew 27:46b).

Anyone who has not felt forsaken of God at least once in his life has not yet lived. Moreover, the pulpit that does not have a sympathetic and suggestive word for our mental and spiritual depressions is not worthy of the name.

Therefore, we leave for a moment the theology of the atonement and look at the Cross of Christ to ask,

"When God seems to 'let us down,' what then?"

I. In the first place, let it be said in no uncertain terms that (whatever divine desertion may have been involved in the suffering Saviourhood of Christ), *when God lets us down, He only* seems *to!* That is to say, our blurred vision and inability to sense Him at the particular moment are not due to God's withdrawal but to our own feelings of aloneness.

For example when in a total eclipse of the sun, darkness broods over the face of the earth, you and I are without light but we know that behind the moon the sun is still shining. Or, on a dreary day, we may feel depressed and say that the sun does not shine, but actually we know that if, even for an hour, the sun withheld entirely its sustaining rays, we poor, puny mortals on this planet would surely freeze to death! So on our depressed days, when God seems to let us down, *our desertion is actually more apparent than real.* When desperation cries,

> "Truth forever on the scaffold, Wrong forever on the throne. . . ."

Faith and Insight whisper,

> "Yet that scaffold sways the future, and, behind the dim unknown,
> Standeth God within the shadows, keeping watch above His own."

Our suffering, however, is nonetheless horrible simply because the desertion is a feeling rather than a fact. Imagined hurts of the mind are often far worse than real pains in the body. Small comfort, then, and idiotic to tell a sufferer his pains are merely "in his head" and imaginary. *Imagination is real to the imaginer!* Therefore, even though in our saner moments we know that God never "lets us down" but only seems to, the suffering is the same. Even apparent divine desertion is bad enough. Each and every one of us must wisely pray,

> "O may no earth-born cloud arise
> To hide Thee from Thy servant's eyes."
> —"Sun of My Soul"
> Hymn, Rev. John Keble, 1820

II. In the second place, then, granting that God never actually lets us down but only seems to (which is almost as bad), let us consider briefly some of the clouds, real or imagined, which blur our vision of God and so depress us.

1. For one thing, when we are depressed and God seems to let us down, we must never forget *the clouds of physical fatigue or pain.* How heavily they hung around the head of the crucified Christ! When He cried,

> "My God, my God, why hast thou forsaken me?"

He had already been a long time upon the cross, and every moment the agony was increasing. As Stalker so graphically puts it,

> "The wounds in His hands and feet, exposed to the atmosphere and the sun, grew scabbed and hardened; the blood, impeded in its circulation, swelled in heart and brain, till these organs were about to burst; and the slightest attempt to move the body from the one intolerable posture caused pains to shoot along quivering nerves. Bodily suffering (real or imagined) clouds the brain and distorts the images on the mirror of the mind. Even the face of God, reflected there, may be turned into a shape of terror by the fumes of physical trouble" — (*The Trial and Death of Jesus Christ,* pp. 231 ff.).

Moreover, the horror of physical suffering may have been greater to Jesus than to ordinary men, because of the fineness and sensitiveness of His physical body. As Stalker continues,

> "His body had never been coarsened with sin, and therefore death was utterly alien to it" – (*Ibid.*, p. 232).

At any rate, you and I know that our so-called paragons of physical perfection, never sick a day in their lives, frequently react violently to pain. Contrary to common opinion, robust health is not always the best discipline for life. In Bulwer-Lytton's memorable phrase:

> "The same refinement which brings us new pleasures exposes us to new pains."

Again, remember that Jesus was not only in physical pain; *He was suffering from physical fatigue*. For three strenuous years He went about giving His life a ransom for many and drinking deeply of the busy cup of salvation. From midnight on Mt. Olive's brow to scorching noon on Calvary's cross it was the same old exhausting business of love laying down itself to lift and to redeem. Small wonder, then, that there came a horrible reaction of sheer physical exhaustion, when the sun was darkened and He recoiled with a loud cry! The clutching fingers of a needy world had tugged so incessantly at the hem of His garment! Now virtue was literally drained out of Him. So, in a lesser degree, many an aggressive preacher or a busy church worker feels forsaken of God on Monday morning. As Evelyn Underhill, the British mystic, once said (in effect),

> "Many a priest has confessed to me that the only thing he is fit for on a Sunday night is a warm bath."

At any rate, when God seems to "let you down," you are probably just tired – weary from either foolish living or from well doing. Don't try to burn the candle at both ends and still feel close to God!

2. Again, when we are depressed and God seems to "let us down," *He may be trying to render us mentally mature.* Many of us need a "cross" to give us a sustaining philosophy of life and to enable us to grow up spiritually. As Francis Bacon said,

> "A little philosophy inclineth a man's mind to atheism, but depth in philosophy bringeth men's minds about to religion."

Ah, but depth in philosophy never comes without a "cross." So

> "Oft the cloud that wraps the present hour
> Serves to brighten all our future days."

For example, some of us sometimes are depressed and feel forsaken of God because of a natural but superficial mental attitude which confuses God with His inadequate ministers and servants. Perhaps, it was the chief priests and elders who, mocking Jesus, made Him feel that established religion was plagued with hypocrites and that, therefore, God must be dead! Alas, many an idealist has confused inadequate church members with an inadequate God. Listen to Hamlet, the young perfectionist and dreamer, disillusioned by the adultery of the mother he adored, making a shallow but natural identification of her sin with God's impotence.

> "O God! O God! How weary, stale, flat, and unprofitable seems to me all the uses of the world!"

His mother "let him down" and immaturely he felt forsaken of God! We say "immaturely," because the Cross is an eternal reminder to teach us that man's inhumanity to man is perhaps permitted of God to purge us of a dollar and cent morality. Perhaps it is best that all men are not dependable and good lest our kindness degenerate into a mere mercenary loving of those who love us. Friends, we are not mentally mature until we rid ourselves of the naive idea that we should be thanked for everything we do. As someone has said,

> "Better to expose ourselves to ingratitude than fail in assisting the unfortunate."

The Cross, then, and its crucified goodness, teaches us that, if we are to keep our reason in a lunatic world, we must not expect wages for our virtue every Saturday night!

3. Again, when we are depressed and God seems to let us down, it may be due not only to physical pain or fatigue — not only to render us mentally mature, but it may be *to show us the dangers of a bad conscience.* For mark it: the pangs of trouble are accentuated and rendered almost unbearable if we have a guilty conscience. When calamity falls on most of us the first thing we say is,

> "What have I done to deserve this?"

Moreover, if we are honest in asking that question, we can generally find something on our consciences to make us feel that maybe our affliction is the avenging hand of God. To be sure, there are morally hardened people with convenient consciences, who would agree with Henrich Heine who said,

> "Psychical pain is more easily borne than physical; and if I had my choice between a bad conscience and a bad tooth, I should choose a bad conscience."

Most of us, however, are like the penitent thief on the cross. Trouble comes and we feel that "we suffer the due reward of our deeds." As Shakespeare says,

> "Conscience doth make cowards of us all."

At any rate, when we are depressed and God seems to "let us down," it is much easier to bear it if, in addition to our external crosses, we are not plagued by the internal gnawings of remorse. Fortunately, for the Christ, He was without blemish and without spot. That made His cross more bearable. Ah, my soul,

> "How blunt are all the arrows of God's quiver in comparison with guilt."

So, wise and good men have long looked on affliction as a school of virtue. It corrects levity and interrupts the confidence of sinning. In trouble and uncertainty we are more receptive to the voice which cries,

> "Come now let us reason together, saith the Lord.
> Though your sins be as scarlet they shall be white like snow.
> Though they be red like crimson, they shall be as wool" (Isaiah 1:18).

Friends, for all our modern slurring of sin and its consequences, anyone who deals intimately with individuals knows that when God seems to "let us down," we stay down, until we learn to say with confidence and faith.

> "I believe in the forgiveness of sins."

What worthwhile person is not forsaken without that?

III. Finally, when God seems to "let us down," we must not only remember that it may be due to physical pain or fatigue, to mental immaturity, or conscious sin; but, above all, *comfort yourself with the assurance that God's apparent desertions are always temporary.* While there is life in your body there is always a second chance. So Jesus passed from depression to quiet confidence again, saying at last,

> "Father, into thy hands, I commend my spirit" (Luke 23:46).

God never "lets us down" permanently. The eternal stars always shine out when it gets dark enough!

Moreover, there is evidence that Jesus' crying,

> "Eli, eli, lama sabachthani,"

did not feel finally forsaken but *only temporarily left on His own!* There are scholars who feel that the words,

> "My God, my God, why hast thou forsaken me?" (Matthew 27:46b).

are too strong a translation of the Aramaic language which Jesus actually used. A missionary familiar with that part of the Orient where a form of Aramaic is still used, tells us that one day he and his wife went out on a preaching tour early in the morning and left their small children alone in the house. They intended to return before dark. When they did not, their children were naturally quite frightened. When, several hours after dark, the parents did return, the children greeted them in Aramaic,

> "Lama sabachthani; lama sabachthani?"

Not, Why have you forsaken us? They knew their parents had not left them permanently. Their use of "Lama sabachthani?" meant,

> "Why have you been away so long?"

Such is the meaning of the Aramaic today. Maybe 2,000 years ago, therefore, Jesus used these words, not when He hung in the depths of depression and despair but when the clouds began to lift and He sensed God's presence again. Maybe it was not rebuke but surprise that the Cross was even more heavy than He had expected.

> "Eli, eli, lama sabachthani?"
>
> *My God, my God, why did you stay away so long?*

When God seems to let us down, what then? The conclusion of the matter is this; We are never allowed to suffer without a purpose. Sometimes it is a divinely permitted discipline to render us mentally mature. Sometimes it is a school of virtue to correct levity and interrupt the confidence of sinning. But always it is God's way of calling us to the strength of His loving arms. As Tennyson put it when at last he regained his faith after deep depression when his young friend Arthur Hallem died,

> "Affliction is the world's altar stairs,
> That slope through darkness up to God."

Or, as we sing in Birdie Bell's poem, "I Have Always Found It So":

> "Never mind the clouds which gather
> O'er the pathway as you go
> Each will have a silver lining,
> I have always found it so!
>
> "Never lose your faith and courage,
> Though the tears may sometimes flow,
> There's a joy for every sorrow,
> I have always found it so.
>
> "Ever keep a heart undaunted,
> Trust the One whose love you know,
> Christ will be your Guide and Saviour,
> I have always found it so.
>
> "Darkest clouds will have a rainbow,
> Light upon your path will glow,
> God is faithful who has promised,
> I have always found it so.
>
> "In the sunshine or the shadow,
> Anywhere He bids you go,
> God is with you as you journey,
> I have always found it so."

Forbid, O God, that we should forget, amid our earthly comforts, the pains and mortal anguish that our Lord Jesus endured for our salvation. Grant us a true vision of all that He suffered, in His betrayal, His lonely agony, His false trial, His mocking and scourging, and the torture of death upon the cross.

As Thou hast given thyself utterly for us, may we give ourselves entirely to Thee, O Jesus Christ, our only Lord and Saviour.

O God, whose only begotten Son followed the way of faith and duty even to the crown of thorns and the cross: Give us grace that we may learn the harder lessons of our faith, and so endue us with power from on high that, taking up our cross in His patience and humility, we may enter into fellowship with His sufferings. Amen

5

On Being Really Human

THE FIFTH WORD

"I thirst." — John 19:28

"As we have therefore opportunity, let us do good unto all men." — Galatians 6:10

> *"That best portion of a good man's life,—*
> *His little nameless, unremembered acts*
> *Of kindness and of love."*
>
> — William Wordsworth

"Whoever gives to one of these little ones even a cup of cold water because he is a disciple, truly, I say to you, he shall not lose his reward." — Matthew 10:42

> *"The cup of water given for Thee,*
> *Still holds the freshness of Thy grace;*
> *Yet long these multitudes to see*
> *The sweet compassion of Thy face."*
>
> — Frank Mason North

> *"If I can stop one heart from breaking,*
> *I shall not live in vain;*
> *If I can ease one life the aching,*
> *Or cool one pain,*
> *Or help one fainting robin*
> *Unto his nest again,*
> *I shall not live in vain."*
>
> — Emily Dickinson

"I shall pass through this world but once. Any good therefore that I can do, or any kindness that I can show to any human being, let me do it now. Let me not defer nor neglect it, for I shall not pass this way again."

— Variously attributed to Victor Hugo, George Eliot, to a Quaker missionary, Stephen Grellet, and to others.

On Being Really Human

". . . If any one thirst, let him come to me and drink . . . out of his heart shall flow rivers of living water."

—John 7:37 ff.

". . . whoever drinks of the water that I shall give him will never thirst; the water that I give him will become in him a spring of water welling up to eternal life." —John 4:14

"After this Jesus, knowing that all was now finished, said (to fulfill the scripture), I thirst." —John 19:28

When our Lord uttered the Fifth Word from the Cross, He had been hanging there for four hours or more! The arrest took place about midnight; the ecclesiastical trial ended before sunrise; the civil trial before Pilate took perhaps from six to nine in the morning or even more than those three hours; and the Crucifixion took place at high noon. From noon until three in the afternoon there was darkness over the face of the earth; and between three in the afternoon and sunset (when the Saturday Sabbath began) the death and burial took place. (See Matthew 27:1; Mark 15:25, 33, 34, and 42.)

The Fourth Word from the Cross,

> "My God, my God, why hast thou forsaken me?" (Matthew 27:46),

marked the climax of the depressed mental anguish of the divine Sufferer during the three hours of silence and darkness which preceded its utterance. This desperate vocalization of His mental and spiritual anguish freed His mind from that mysterious struggle. This view is confirmed by the phrase with which John, who witnessed the agony, introduces the Fifth Word,

> "After this, Jesus, knowing that all was now finished, said (to fulfill the scripture), 'I thirst'" (John 19:28).

The phrase "to fulfill the scripture" is often interpreted as if the meaning were that our Lord dutifully said this Fifth Word, "I thirst," in fulfillment of some prediction that He would do so; and the Old Testament is ransacked, without much result, for the prophecy alluded to. It is better, however, to connect this phrase about Scripture fulfillment with what goes just before it, namely,

> ". . . Jesus, knowing that all was now finished . . ."

It was only when His work, appointed by God and prescribed in Scripture, was completed, that He became sufficiently conscious of His bodily condition to say, "I thirst."

We all know how intense mental and spiritual preoccupation can make us oblivious to bodily wants. Reading a fascinating book often makes us forget food or sleep. Those of us who love to study and write may go for hours without noting that we are hungry and thirsty and actually dead tired. During the forty days and nights of Temptation in the wilderness Jesus was too absorbed with mental and spiritual struggle to be aware of His bodily needs, but when the spiritual strain was removed, we read that "afterward he was hungry" (Matthew 4:2b).

At Jacob's Well in Samaria our Lord's preoccupied concern with helping the sinful Samaritan woman not only made Him forget to eat but actually nourished Him. It is written that

> ". . . the disciples besought him, saying, 'Rabbi, eat.' But he said to them, 'I have food to eat of which you do not know. . . . My food is to do the will of him who sent me, and to accomplish his work" (John 4:31 ff.).

To accomplish His work? Yes, on the Cross our Lord not only poured out His life blood to save us all, but He also poured out His love to pray for His persecutors, to pardon the pentitent thief, and to make provision for His widowed mother in the home of His beloved disciple, John! So much "virtue went out of Him" that He sank for a season into deep mental and spiritual depression, crying,

> "My God, my God, why hast thou forsaken me?" (Matthew 27:46).

But now . . . and now only . . . when His redemptive work in general and His redemptive acts in particular were finished and done . . . did He utter *the only cry of* physical *pain made upon the cross!*

> "After this, Jesus, knowing that all was now finished, said (to fulfill by Scripture), 'I thirst' " (John 19:28).

The Scripture fulfilment refers to God's promised redemption in Christ and not to the cry, "I thirst." Only when God's redemptive purpose had been accomplished, did our Lord permit Himself to think of His burning thirst!

James Stalker says,

"I remember once talking with a German student who had served in the Franco-Prussian War. He was wounded in an engagement near Paris, and lay on the field unable to stir. He did not know exactly what was the nature of his wound, and he thought he might be dying. The pain was intense; the wounded and dying were groaning round about him; the battle was still raging; and shots were falling and tearing up the ground in all directions. But after a time, one agony (he told me) began to swallow up all the rest, and soon made him forget his wound, his danger and his neighbors. It was the agony of thirst. He would have given the world for a draught of water" – (*Trial and Death of Jesus Christ*, pp. 242 ff.).

Many of us regularly gave blood to the Red Cross during World War II and even now, on occasion, give blood to our church account in the Blood Bank at a hospital. When it is over, the refreshing drink they give us fulfils our deepest need and desire of that moment. So there is a sense in which thirst was the supreme distress of the Crucifixion. The agonies of nails in hands and feet . . . with body weight tearing and tugging at throbbing wounds . . . were horrible and excruciating; but, after a time, the pain was lost and swallowed up in overpowering thirst and our Lord permitted Himself to be *supremely human* and cry for all to hear,

"I thirst" (John 19:28).

I. Note, in the first place, that *this pathetic cry seems surprising on the lips of the Son of God.* Can this be the confident Christ who, standing in Jerusalem, not long before, said to the multitude,

". . . If any one thirst, let him come to me and drink . . . out of his heart shall flow rivers of living water" (John 7:37).

Can this be He who, standing at the well of Jacob, said to the Samaritan woman,

> ". . . whoever drinks of the water that I shall give him will never thirst; the water that I give him will become in him a spring of water welling up to eternal life" (John 4:14).

Yes, this pathetic cry seems surprising on the lips of the Son of God, but it is just the typical contrast between His inner wealth and outer poverty! St. Paul saw this when He wrote to the Church at Corinth,

> ". . . you know the grace of our Lord Jesus Christ, that though he was rich, yet for your sake he became poor, so that by his poverty you might be rich" (II Corinthians 8:9).

As the old gospel song sings it,

> "Out of the ivory palaces, into the world of woe,
> Only His great redeeming love made my Saviour
> go."

He was able to enrich the whole world, yet He had to be supported by the contributions of the women who followed Him. Luke, who so strongly portrays for rugged Romans our Lord as the ideal man, writes,

> ". . . the twelve were with him, and also some women who . . . provided for them [Jesus and the disciples] out of their means" (Luke 8:1 ff.).

He could say, "I am the Bread of Life" yet He sometimes hungered for a meal; He could promise "thrones and many mansions" to those who believe on Him, yet He said of Himself,

> "Foxes have holes, and the birds of the air have nests,

> yet the Son of man hath not where to lay his head" (Luke 9:58).

Yes, there was more truth than cruel mockery in the derision of the hostile chief priests and scribes and elders who taunted Him on Calvary, sneering,

> "He saved others; he cannot save himself" (Matthew 27:42a).

Surprisingly human and pathetic? No, the good news of the gospel insists that God had to become really human to redeem us. Listen again to John, his cousin whose mother Salome was the Virgin Mary's sister,

> "In the beginning was the word, and the Word was with God, and the Word was God" (John 1:1).

> "And the Word became flesh and dwelt among us, full of grace and truth; we have beheld his glory, glory as of the only Son from the Father . . . and from his fulness have we all received, grace upon grace. For the law was given through Moses; grace and truth came through Jesus Christ" (John 1:14 ff.).

Yes, *surprisingly human but not pathetic!* The Word of God created the heavens and the earth! The Word of God was in the Ten Commandments from Moses! But, according to the Gospel, the Word of God had to stoop to conquer! God does not shout to us from a Throne. He stoops to us to "thirst" on a Cross. Writing to persecuted Christians scattered abroad and tempted to defect from the faith, the author of Hebrews pleads,

> "Since then we have a great high priest who has passed through the heavens, Jesus, the Son of God, let us hold fast our confession. For we have not a high priest who is unable to sympathize with our weaknesses, but who

in every respect has been tempted as we are, yet without sinning. Let us then with confidence draw near to the throne of grace, that we may receive mercy and find grace to help in time of need" (Hebrews 4:14-16).

The Son of God had to become really human to help us! Years ago in New Jersey I had a dedicated member and friend who nevertheless dismissed most of Jesus' idealistic teachings saying,

> "Of course, He can do it and did it. He is Divine. But you and I are human; we can't even approximate His impossible ideals."

Some years ago we were called from Pittsburgh, Pennsylvania, to Richmond, Virginia, and had to change denominational label from so-called "northern" to "southern" Presbyterian. At that time our "northern" church was suspect in wide areas of the South as more liberal in theology than the "southern" church. Therefore, I stood before East Hanover Presbytery in Richmond expecting to be examined rigorously to see if I believed in the Divinity of Christ. To my surprise, the questions all assumed that, coming from conservative Pittsburgh, I might overemphasize Christ's Divinity at the expense of His Real Humanity! They asked me only to state my faith about the Real Humanity of Jesus and, when convinced that I did accept the mystery of the Incarnation, the Chairman on Examinations said,

> "We fooled you, didn't we? You thought we would hunt only heresy on the 'left' and we are equally concerned with heresy on the 'right' which denies that our Lord was 'tempted in all points like we are' and on the Cross cried out, 'I thirst.' "

II. In the second place, note that *God does not "talk down" to us in a haughty creed; he "comes down" to us in a humble life!* He is Emmanuel – God with us. This is sound psychology. We humans, young and old, hate to be "talked down to."

Some years ago I visited in a home where a young girl, aged ten, received me and delighted me with adult conversation until her mother came down from upstairs. One thing that little girl said I shall never forget,

> "You know [she said] I knew a minister once who was a good and a smart man, but he 'burned me up' when he would put his hand on my head and say, 'Bless you, my child.' "

God is not like that minister. *God does not "talk down" to us; in Christ He "comes down" to us in a humble life!*

How wise God is! For we are all children – spiritually. I am still smoldering from an experience I had when just out of Princeton Seminary. An older minister, aged thirty-five, who had not seen me since high school days, now saw me at the age of twenty-four and said,

> "My boy, you have grown since I saw you last."

When will preachers learn that the good God and good men never "talk down" to us; like our Lord they must come down to "live where we are," and we love and follow them to the ends of the earth!

We repeat:

> "The Word of God was in the Ten Commandments. The Word of God was in the voice of the stern prophets. But the Word had to stoop to conquer us. In Jesus 'the Word became flesh and dwelt among us.' "

But, alas, we poor mortals have mistaken notions of Divinity. Too often we think only of majesty and miracles. Like the shepherds of old we tremble before heavenly hosts and are sore afraid. But God reassures us, saying,

> "Be not afraid; for behold, I bring you good news of a great joy . . . for unto you is born . . . a Saviour, who is Christ the Lord" (Luke 2:10-11).

A Saviour? Christ the Lord? Yes but

> "They were looking for a King
> To raise their hopes and lift them high;
> Then came a little baby thing
> That made a woman cry!"

In that Manger Child was the Word of God in a whisper — a whisper that would grow and grow into a saving Voice that would shake the world with the power of the Almighty! But, you see, God did not thunder from His throne. He comes down to "hunger and thirst" with us in a real life and death upon the Cross!

Indeed, many do not believe in the Divinity of Jesus because they start out with wrong notions of real Divinity. Gabriel, in the Negro spiritual drama by Marc Connelly called "The Green Pastures," is a case in point. Remember how in an early scene of that famous play, Gabriel, a pompous, King-fish sort of a character as the Archangel, struts into the heavenly fish fry and lords it over the lesser angels, crying,

> "Gang-way for the Lord God Almighty!"

Unless you have seen the play and caught its informal, Negro spiritual manner, that sounds like blasphemy. But, above all, it reveals our typical ignorance of real Divinity. For when God does walk out on that stage, Who is He? The Lord God Almighty? No, just a humble old preacher with the light of Christ in his eyes!

Yes, even a dramatist like Marc Connelly caught the truth

we theologians and ministers often miss. *God does not "talk down" to us.* In Jesus Christ *God "comes down" to live and die for you and me!*

Too often folks put preachers on a pious pedestal and forget the simple gospel truth that Jesus, the greatest Preacher who ever lived, was Human and approachable. Our Lord was not everlastingly worried about his dignity. He was big enough to be small enough to be used! Yet listen to an ancient creed about Christ:

> "Two whole, perfect and distinct natures, the Godhead and the manhood, were inseparably joined together in one person, without conversion, composition, or confusion. Which person is very God and very man, yet one Christ, the only Mediator between God and man."

Friends, in all reverence I believe that; but, heaven help me, I resent the haughty non-Biblical language of some of our creeds! To be sure, such creeds have the good intention of trying to express the inexpressible, but creeds can "talk down" to us if they are not Biblical in simple language!

Here is the good news! *God does not "talk down" to us in a creed: He comes down to us in "a hungering and thirsting" life,* saying,

> "Suffer the little children to come unto me . . ." (Matthew 10:14).
> "Except ye become as a little child, ye cannot enter the Kingdom of God" (Mark 10:15).

Take God at His word. He knows from Incarnate experience. To break through to our spiritual childishness even God himself had to be born again in a manger!

III. In the third place, note that *in our Lord's very human appeal for a drink we have a supreme example of his undying faith in sinners like you and me.* On the Cross it would have been so easy for Him to have wrapped the mantle of self-righteousness around Him. Surely, the Roman soldiers who nailed Him to the Cross were hopeless and beyond redemption. Those efficient executioners, so brutalized by their business that, like vultures, they calmly gambled for His clothing – surely, these callous and cruel specialists in crucifixion could be dismissed by our Lord as "impossible"!

But, friends, underline this indelibly in our Christian thinking. Christ sees much in this world to weep over and much more to pray over, but He sees nothing in this world to look upon with contempt as beyond redemption. On the Cross He was surrounded by those who had wantonly wronged Him; not only had they inflicted pain, but they had mocked and laughed at His sufferings. You and I would have resolved to die rather than show our feelings; at least, we would have died rather than have asked of these brutes a kindness. But listen to the record:

> "After this [that is to say, after all that men had done to Him] Jesus said . . . 'I thirst' " (John 19:28).

The wonder of it! Not only did He ask a favor; *He expected to receive it!* Shamefully as He had been treated by those to whom He had to appeal, He believed there was still some milk of human kindness even in the hard-hearted Roman executioners; and *He was not disappointed!* It is written that

> "A jar of sour wine was sitting there, so a sponge was soaked in it and put on a hyssop branch and held up to His lips" (John 19:29, *The Living New Testament*).

Unfortunately, some of our English translations say that they gave Him "vinegar" so that their action has been interpreted as one which added insult to injury. Actually, however, these rough soldiers shared with Jesus some of the sour Italian wine so sure to be in the canteen of a Roman soldier – or in a jar nearby for men on duty. Scholars are correct in saying that *this sour wine* or "vinegar" (as it was called in the 1611 English of the King James Version) *was to a sufferer a refreshing drink.* Even on the Cross He asked a favor expectantly, saying,

> "I thirst" (John 19:28).

and in the soldiers' action His confidence was justified!

What an undying faith in sinners like you and me! What a tragedy that in His hour of thirst Jesus had no disciples close enough to the Cross to give Him a drink! He had to throw Himself on the mercy of pagan strangers. This sad commentary on life has disillusioned a great multitude which no man can number. As one embittered friend puts it,

> "I find more understanding and forgiveness in a tavern than in the average church."

We have reason to believe our Lord died of a "broken heart" – a heart broken by the so-called "best people" who, because of fear, forsook Him rather than stand up and be counted when "the going got rough." Nicodemus might have used his religious intellect for the Kingdom, but He was afraid of what intellectuals (?) might think; so he came to see Jesus under the cover of darkness. The rich young ruler might have dedicated his wealth to support the costly cause for which Jesus stands; he was a lovable sort, but

> ". . . he went away sorrowful because he was very rich" (Luke 18:23).

The Holy City, whose inhabitants our Lord longed to gather under His wing, joined with those who mocked Him on the Cross. No wonder, then, when they pierced His side water came out mingled with blood! (John 19:34). Doctors say this is a sign of a ruptured . . . broken heart!

Suffice it to say, it is hard to face life in the raw and still expect the best from sinners like you and me. There is no more difficult business in the world. But, friends, it is a thrilling business! Nothing is exciting about a safe bet and a "sure thing" that succeeds every time! Of course, kindness and "turning the other cheek" do not work every time. Jesus chose not to defend Himself and so remained silent at His trial. His forgiveness, however, did not turn them from their evil purpose! But He knows that *unkindness and dragging others down with violent words and actions never succeeds in the long run!* The human mind is so constructed that it resists rigor and yields to softness in the end. And so-called "softness" is not weak! Power can do by gentleness that which violence always fails to accomplish. Kindness, over the centuries, has converted more sinners than reforming zeal, eloquence, or learning!

And, mark it, the Christian who has never won an enemy with kindness has never really lived. As Jesus put it concerning the adulterous woman of Samaria, who approached Him with century old prejudice against Jews but was finally won by quiet patience and the unexpected asking for the favor of a drink,

> "I have food to eat of which you do not know . . ." (John 4:32).

Sometimes I think this business of being a Christian in our relations with others is like aviation. Every so often a plane falls. More often in our flights into the atmosphere of helpfulness and good will we get "let down" with a crippling crash. The true flier, however, always goes up again as soon as he gets a chance! What if we Christians, even on a "cross," would grasp the first opportunity to go right on asking for – and expecting the best in people – in Jesus' name!

Our Father, whose Son died upon the Cross, suffering a burning thirst, enable us truly to hunger and thirst after a right relation with Thee that we might make more right our relations with others and be increasingly filled with the water of life.

The deer is panting for a stream and our hearts are athirst for Thee, even when we know it not.

Thou has made us for Thyself so that our hearts are always restless until we find ourselves in the undiscourageable Love of Jesus Christ, our Lord. Amen

6

Secrets of Satisfied Living

THE SIXTH WORD

"It is finished!" — John 19:30

*"The journey is done. . . . O thou Soul of my soul!
I shall clasp Thee again."* — Robert Browning

"Be not grieved above measure for thy deceased friends. They are not dead, but have only finished the journey which it is necessary for every one of us to take."

— Antiphanes

"Our friend and we were invited abroad to a party of pleasure, which is to last forever. His chair was ready first, and he is gone before us. We could not all conveniently start together; and why should you and I be grieved at this, since we are soon to follow, and know where to find him.

— Benjamin Franklin

"Good-night! Good-night! as we so oft have said,
Beneath this roof at midnight, in the days
That are no more, and shall no more return.
Thou hast but taken up thy lamp and gone to bed;
I stay a little longer, as one stays
To cover up the embers that still burn."

—Henry Wadsworth Longfellow
(Whose wife accidentally fell
into the fireplace and burned to death)

"I have fought the good fight, I have finished the race, I have kept the faith. Henceforth there is laid up for me the crown of righteousness, which the Lord, the righteous judge, will award to me on that Day, and not only to me but also to all who have loved his appearing."

— St. Paul to young Timothy
(II Timothy 4:7-8)

Secrets of Satisfied Living

"When, therefore, Jesus had received the sour wine, he said, It is finished" – John 19:30

In the Greek language in which the New Testament is written it takes only a single word to express the idea which we in English translate,

> *"It is finished";*

and it is the greatest single word ever uttered. *"It is finished"* – that one word in Greek or that one phrase in English – may be said to comprehend in itself the salvation of the world; and thousands of human souls, in the joy of being forgiven, or in the crisis of death, have laid hold upon its promise as the drowning sailor grasps the life line.

Of course, it may be that we Christians habitually read too much into every word which fell from the lips of our Lord. The phrase, *"It is finished"* (so some suggest) may have been merely the death rattle of an ebbing life, as if the meaning were,

> "It is all over! The last agony of pain and weakness is ended at last!"

Thus the meaning is a *cry of relief*:

> "Thank God, it is finished and the time has come 'to shuffle off this mortal coil'! It is a consumation devoutly to be wished!"

Yet a closer look at the record convinces us that this dying word of Jesus was not spoken in a whipped and broken tone. The Fifth Sentence from the Cross ("I thirst"), we are expressly told, was uttered with *a loud voice;* so was the Seventh Sentence ("Father, into Thy hands I commend my spirit"); and, although this is not expressly stated about the Sixth Sentence ("It is finished"), it is likely that it also, falling in between, was also spoken in a strong voice. At any rate, *"It is finished"* is not a cry of defeated relief; *it is a shout of victory!*

This conviction is enhanced by the fact that as soon as Jesus bowed His head and "gave up the ghost," the rugged Roman in charge of the crucifixion was so impressed with the majesty of our Lord's passing that He cried,

> "Truly [this was a righteous man . . . surely,] this was the Son of God" (Matthew 20:28).

My friends, that burly Roman, who knew a real man when he saw one, was convinced that this was no cringing death of dismay and defeat. He had seen with his own eyes and heard with his own ears the triumph of which Rousseau later wrote,

> "If Socrates died like a sage, Jesus died like a God!"

"It is finished," then, was not a cry of devastated despair but rather an expression of satisfied achievement. And the question at once arises: What was the achievement whose completion brought such comfort and courage to the Christ? *What are the secrets of satisfied living?*

Of course, in all humility and reverence it must be said

at once that no human mind will ever fathom the full meaning of the work which was finished by that "wondrous Cross on which the Prince of Glory died." There are more things in heaven and earth than are dreamed of in any church's theology. The ocean of God's love is so very wide and deep, and our little boats of faith are so very small! But the vastness of the ocean of mystery has not kept devout men and women from sailing their mental boats and consequently there are many theological theories as to what was finished on that far-off day when the Master

> "looked upon the travail of his soul and was satisfied" (Isaiah 53:11).

I. In the first place, then, let us look at *some of the more familiar theories of the atonement* which have been taught by the church throughout the centuries.

1. For one thing, there are *the ransom theories of the atonement* which say that on the cross Christ finished buying back sinful humanity from either the imprisoning wrath of a righteously indignant God or from the enslaving bondage of a powerfully tenacious Devil. That is to say, on Calvary Christ paid for us a ransom either to God or to Satan. To be sure, these ransom theories are a bit picturesque to the modern mind, but the Scripture does make it plain that Calvary reveals both God's sacrificial hatred of sin and the Devil's malignancy and persistent power. So, says the Bible,

> ". . . the Son of man came not to be served but to serve, and to give His life as *a ransom for many*" (Matthew 20:28).

2. Again, there is the so-called *governmental theory of the atonement,* first enunciated by Hugo Grotius, the Dutch expert on international law, who said that God had to

crucify His Son to warn anarchistic men that in the divine government of the world no evil can ever go unpunished without weakening the law. Moreover, the innocent often suffer for the lawlessness of the guilty. You see, long before Moses had spoken of God as One,

> "who will by no means clear the guilty" (Exodus 34:7).

and

> "visiting the iniquity of the fathers upon the children. . ." (Exodus 34:7).

Thus, said Grotius, the righteous Ruler of the world could not let sin go unpunished lest the law be flaunted (as it is in our time). According to Grotius God took out His sense of justice upon the innocent Christ!

3. Then there are the more popular *moral influence theories of the atonement,* all of which wax eloquent over the uplifting example of both divine and human goodness which cares enough to lay down its life that others might live! As a matter of fact, nothing hits so hard and lifts us so high as the love and courage of someone who cares enough to suffer for us. There is always a magnetism in unselfish service. As Jesus Himself put it,

> "And, I, if I be lifted up, will draw all men unto myself" (John 12:32).

4. Then, once more, there are the *substitutionary views of the atonement,* perhaps the most prominent in Presbyterian theology, which insists that on the Cross Christ *in our stead* gave the perfect obedience which God requires of us all, and *in our place* He paid the penalty for our sinful inability to obey! This, too, is Scriptural,

> "He was wounded for our transgressions; He was bruised for our iniquities. The chastisement of our

> peace was upon Him, and with His stripes we are healed" (Isaiah 53:5).

Thus we have ransom theories, governmental theories, moral influence theories, and substitutionary theories of the atonement! And to the reverent mind there is *truth in them all!* The more one goes into the experience of the good men who proclaimed these theories in the first place, the more he is inclined to accept them all. But, just as no great human experience can be adequately dismissed by definitions or finally frozen into a formal formula, so the Cross, this greatest of Divine Experiences, cannot be finally "tied up with blue ribbon" and "delivered post paid" to any generation or individual! The Cross is "beyond our poor powers to add or subtract!"

At any rate, the Bible narrative makes it plain that Jesus Himself looked upon both His life and death as of tremendous importance for the world. The first secret of His satisfied living lay in *his sense of being charged of God with a task!* In the Temple at the age of twelve He is even then "about his Father's business" (Luke 2:49). By the well of Samaria He redeems a fallen woman and rebukes His prudish disciples, saying,

> "I have meat to eat that you know not of" (John 4:32).

> "My meat is to do the will of him that sent me, and to finish his work" (John 4:34).

In the Upper Room on the eve of Crucifixion He prays to God,

> "I have glorified Thee on the earth:
> I have finished the work Thou gavest me to do"
> (John 17:4).

This, then, was the task of the Master — *to glorify God on the earth* — to make known the Father to the sons of men!

This bringing of God to men and men to God began in Bethlehem's Babe and continued in the Nazareth boy. On Calvary's Cross He could confidently say of this reconciling and redemptive work,

"It is finished!" (John 19:30b).

In the service of God and in behalf of men He felt the satisfaction of a work well done!

II. In the second place, however, leaving theology for a moment, consider how in these victorious words, *"It is finished,"* there is the satisfaction of One who has *solved the age old problem of human suffering.* On the Cross our Lord demonstrated that God sometimes washes our eyes with tears in order that we may read more clearly His providence and His commandments. In a word, when Jesus said, *"It is finished,"* He was forever satisfied that the Cross was not only sin's will, or His enemies' will, but also God's will and plan for His life!

No one of us is ever satisfied with life until his faith is strong enough to accept life's inevitable pains as the mysterious yet ultimately benevolent will of God! No Christian character is finished until,

"however, bitter the cup we have to drink, we are sure it contains nothing unnecessary or unkind."

To be sure, there are many who bear their "crosses" stoically in the stolid conviction that God has nothing to do with them. These are good people who think it is disrespectful to God to think of Him even as One who permits evil for our ultimate good. Therefore, they rebel at sudden and tragic death and recoil at their comforters who make the old Prayer Book's complacent assurance that it

". . . has pleased Almighty God to take out of the world the soul of our brother departed."

One December dusk many years ago in Cleveland Heights, Ohio, a favorite uncle of mine was driving his car in a blinding blizzard when he struck an unmarked street car pole and was instantly killed. He had been for years a teacher of a huge Men's Bible Class and a tither who gave away most of his income to church and charity. It was my difficult assignment not only to identify him at the morgue but also to conduct his funeral. The widow, my aunt, a devout church member all her life, had but one request. She said,

> "Clem, whatever you say, don't use that usual formula about 'it pleasing Almighty God to take out of the world the soul of our brother departed.' No [she cried], God had nothing to do with this! It was a cruel accident caused by a blizzard, the street car company's criminal negligence in having an unmarked black pole in the middle of a boulevard, and by Wes's bad habit of driving too fast in the outside lane. Never try to tell me that God is responsible for the death of a good man."

It was useless to try to tell her that God planned and permitted the cruel and untimely death of Jesus. It would not have helped to quote Peter on the Day of Pentecost, the birthday of the Christian Church,

> "— this Jesus, delivered up according to the definite plan and foreknowledge of God, you crucified and killed by the hands of lawless men" (Acts 2:23).

Moreover, we who have walked through the valley of the shadow, as I did when cancer took my wonderful Christian mother at age 46, can all sympathize with my Aunt Ida's puzzlement. We can even heartily commend her desire to rush to the defense of God by absolving him of all blame, including the Divine permission. Yet, friends, anyone who deals intimately with troubled souls knows that, when we really feel that anything whatsoever can happen contrary to the control and permission of God, we are of all men most miserable. Even when a sufferer cannot see in his particular "cross" the will of God, He ought to wish that he could be so "reconciled"! In the words of the melancholy Cowper, so distressed by mysterious Providence that he was plagued by thoughts of suicide,

> "Happy the man who sees a God employed
> In all the good and *ill* that checkers life."

No, it is never easy to face a "cross"! But it is a great thing, when our Gethsemane hours come, when the cup of bitterness is pressed to our lips, and when we pray that it may pass away, to feel that it is not fate – that it is not cruel necessity but Divine Love for *good ends* working mysteriously upon us! Friends, life can never be abundantly satisfying until we stubbornly believe that someway, somehow, *God overrules all mutinous accidents,* brings them under His laws, *and makes them all serve his larger plan!*

To attain this faith we must think of suffering, deserved or undeserved, as a God-given stimulus to greater sympathy and service. We never know how to feel for others and help them unless we ourselves have experienced "the dark line in God's face." Certainly no preacher ever reaches the zenith of his usefulness until he experiences somewhere along the way a broken heart,

> "The good are better made by ill,
> As roses crushed are sweeter still."

As someone has wisely said,

> "To have a true idea of man or of life, one must have stood himself on the brink of suicide, or on the doorsill of insanity, at least once."

Suffering, individual or social, is never satisfactorily borne until it is accepted as the will of God. This is not to recommend a fanatical martyr complex – that false fire of overheated minds. Nor is it an idle, do-nothing, passive fatalism, but a patient confidence in an Almighty Plan.

Such satisfying confidence in the ultimate goodness of God shines supreme from the Cross of Christ. It is a major secret of His satisfied living. For, mark it: the life of Christ was hemmed in and crushed on every side. Evil men were the immediate, close-at-hand cause of His suffering, but He acknowledged behind "the hands of lawless men" the will of God. The Cross was Christ's path to larger service in heaven and on earth. He accepted a career of shame instead of glory, of brief and limited activity instead of the far-travelled beneficence of which his followers dreamed. He had to endure premature, unjust, and violent death instead of world-wide and everlasting empire. But He never murmured by reflecting that *it was the will of his Father that he depart for larger service on Calvary!* When the worst came to the worst, and in Gethsemane he was forced to cry

> "O, my Father, if it be possible, let this cup pass from me" (Matthew 26:39a),

He was swift to add,

> "Nevertheless, not my will, but thine, be done" (Matthew 26:39b).

And thus step after step on the ladder of faith His thoughts were brought into perfect accord with His Father's will. His will was at last by prayer in tune with God!

The conclusion of the matter is this: Jesus found life satisfying because of two major things: He performed His work as sacred service to God. He, therefore, was able to take mysterious suffering as part of His Divine mission. You and I cannot do this unless we really love the work we stand for more than we love our own personal fate! As John, the beloved disciple put it — John who alone stood by at the cross —

> "There is no fear in love, but perfect love casteth out fear" (I John 4:18).

As Ednah D. Cheney sings in her poem called, "The Larger Prayer"

"At first I prayed for Light:
Could I but see the way,
How gladly, swiftly would I walk
To everlasting day!

"And next I prayed for Strength
That I might tread the road
With firm, unfaltering feet, and win
The heaven's serene abode.

"And then I asked for Faith:
Could I but trust my God,
I'd live enfolded in His peace,
Though foes were all abroad.

"But now I pray for Love:
Deep love to God and man,
A living love that will not fail,
However dark His plan.

"And Light and Strength and Faith
Are opening everywhere;
God waited till I prayed for Love
And prayed the larger prayer."

The Best Loved Religious Poems,
Fleming H. Revell Co., 1933, p. 123

Bring us, O God to the end of each day with a sense of having finished something worthwhile for Thee. Help us, we pray Thee, to fight the good fight and keep the faith in spite of the heavy burden of the unaccomplished. The days are not long enough, O Lord, but the weeks are – if we live one day at a time in the simple faith of those who work for others in Thy name and in the steadfast Spirit of Christ Jesus our Lord. Amen

7

The Safest Deposit of All

THE SEVENTH WORD

"Father, into thy hands I commend my spirit."
— Luke 23:46

"The Lord is my shepherd; I shall not want. . . . Yea, though I walk through the valley of the shadow of death, I will fear no evil; for Thou art with me. . . . Surely goodness and mercy shall follow me all the days of my life: And I will dwell in the house of the Lord forever. — Psalm 23

"The Lord is my strength and my shield; my heart trusteth in Him, and I am helped." — Psalm 28:7

"My peace I give unto you. . . . Let not your heart be troubled, neither let it be afraid." — John 14:27

"No coward soul is mine,
No trembler in the world's storm-troubled sphere;
I see heaven's glories shine,
And faith shines equal, arming me from fear."
— Emily Bronte

"Whatever happens, abide steadfast in a determination to cling simply to God." — Francis de Sales

"Don't let this get you down. Just remember that God will make everything right and that I'll see you all again in the hereafter. . . . Read 'Thanitopsis' by Bryant if you want to know how I am taking this. My faith in God is complete, so I am unafraid."
— William G. Farrow, a young Lieutenant, one of three Doolittle fliers condemned to death

The Safest Deposit of All

"Father, into thy hands I commend my spirit."
— Luke 23:46

In this chapter the last words of the dying Christ have guided our thought. We come now to the seventh and last sentence from the Cross,

> "Father, into thy hands I commend my spirit" (Luke 23:46).

And, inasmuch as the word "commend" in the original Greek of the New Testament has in it the idea of "the banking trust of a confident depositor," we might more accurately translate our text,

> "Father, into Thy hands I deposit my spirit" (Luke 23:46).

Therefore, we chose as our seventh and final chapter: *"The Safest Deposit of All"* or *"The Fine Art of Banking on God."*

But, someone asks, "Is not this banking on God an idle fatalism which no resolute man of action can accept?"

To which we answer, "Upon the contrary, banking on

God is something we all must do whether we like it or not."

There are so many things in daily life beyond our human control. For example, we never know (Do we?) when we start out in the morning what will befall us or our loved ones before the day is done? All too often we feel ourselves but actors in an impromptu drama by a mysterious playwright, and, alas, the surprise roles He thrusts upon us persuade us of a "destiny that shapes our ends, rough hew them how we may!" Even those who are not religious one day sooner or later find themselves in the valley of discouragement or death, and we all understand what Charles Wesley meant when he prayed to God in the hymn, "Jesus, Lover of My Soul,"

> "Other refuge have I none; hangs my helpless soul on Thee;
> Leave, ah, leave me not alone, Still support and comfort me!
> All my trust on Thee is stayed, all my help from thee I bring;
> Cover my defenseless head with the shadow of Thy wing."

To be sure, when we are young and in our prime, we may entertain the cocksure notion that we are the sole captains of our fate and that it's altogether up to us to sink or swim, live or die, survive or perish. But, sooner or later, "the slings and arrows of outrageous fortune" convince us of our need of the Everlasting Arms! In spite of our firm-jawed determination there are too many daily happenings over which we exercise little or no control! Whether we like it or not, we are forced to bank on something or someone outside of ourselves!

The question, therefore, is not whether we shall bank on God, but rather *on what kind of a God are we banking?* Obviously we cannot handle all the currency of our living;

we have to deposit some of our destiny on faith. Consciously or unconsciously, every human being commits his uncertainties to some kind of a god. And the kind of a God we bank on, be it blind fate or benevolent Father, determines the quality of our living and the quantity of our courage!

With this much preparation for our thought, then, we turn to study in some detail the fine art of banking not merely on a god but on the Christian God — *the God and Father of our Lord Jesus Christ* — the One to whom on the cruel Cross He confidently prayed,

> "Father, into Thy hands I *deposit* my spirit" (Luke 23:46).

I. In the first place, let it be emphatically said that *we Christians bank our lives not on a blind fate but on the Benevolent Father.* In spite of the difficulties and the daily happenings which seem to deny it, a real Christian keeps unfaltering trust that he lives in a Fatherly universe — whose Creator and Sustainer cares for every individual soul!

For example, in Jesus' seventh sentence from the Cross, we know that He was quoting from Psalm 31:5 which says,

> "Into thy hands I commit my spirit; thou hast redeemed me, O Lord God of truth" (Psalm 31:5).

And we notice at once that in quoting the ancient Psalm the Master left off the last phrase about redemption and added the prefacing word, "Father."

> "Father, into thy hands I commend my spirit" (Luke 23:46).

That word "Father" is not in the old Psalm 31. It could not have been. In Old Testament times the individual had not yet begun to address God as Father, although God was sometimes called the Father of the nation as a whole. You see, Jesus was the first to experience and the first to teach God as the Father of each individual; and ever since, we Christians, in Jesus' name, have banked on a Fatherly God!

And yet for Jesus to talk about a Fatherly God as He hangs on the Cross seems at first sight to be a crazy leap of unfounded faith. It is hard to imagine anything less "fatherly" to the body and spirit of Jesus than the cruel Cross! So for us, too, it is often desperately difficult to think of God as good. More often than we like to admit life's cruelties force us to be but stubborn depositors like the suffering Job who defended his God, saying with his chin out,

> "Though he slay me, yet will I trust him," (Job 13:15a).

In other words, we ministers sometimes make the mistake of trying in every instance to argue desperate folks into accepting God as Father. Alas, there are often tragic times when we do well to keep people believing in God at all — let alone think of Him as Father! Emerson was right when he said,

> "Providence has a wild, rough, incalculable road to its ends, and it is no use to try to whitewash its huge mixed instrumentalities, or to dress up that terrific benefactor in the clean shirt and white collar of a student for the ministry."

Yes, it is difficult to call God "Father" from a Cross — difficult for Christ and harder still for us!

Let it be frankly admitted, then, that our Christian faith in God's Fatherhood is very much like our reception of a distant musical program over the radio! Sometimes reception is clear and sometimes full of static. There are times when the goodness of God falls upon our ears in accents strong and clear. But, alas, there are other times when the storms rage and the lightning crackles in the air. And in stormy hours it takes the magic eye of faith and the patient turning of prayer to render our recognition of God as something other than the static sound of which Shakespeare spoke when he said that life often seems,

> ". . . a tale told by an idiot,
> Full of sound and fury,
> Signifying nothing."

At any rate, be sure of this: Jesus' faith in a fatherly universe was not born on the Cross. It was a banking trust maintained in spite of the panic of the Cross. It was the inevitable climax of a life-time of small deposits. All His days and nights He had walked and talked with God as His Father. His continuing to do so even in death was but the last link in a cable of habit into which He had woven a prayerful thread each day until on the cross it became so strong He could not break it. Not even on the Cross could our Lord call God anything but Father.

> "Father, into Thy hands I deposit my spirit" (Luke 23:46).

Thus we hear him saying in effect,

> "Father, I have made such deposits daily for years; I do it now for eternity."

II. In the second place, however, someone is sure to be thinking, "How did Jesus keep alive — day in and day out — His faith in God as Father?" The answer is simple: He did what every church member promises to do when he unites with a Presbyterian church (and with most others). *He made "diligent use of the means of grace"!* In that old fashioned phrase of our forefathers we find Jesus' secret of staying power. He made "diligent use of the means of grace." That is to say, besides listening to regular preaching and teaching in the synagogue or temple, *he read the Bible and prayed every day!* You see, there is no magic shortcut to spiritual power. Faith is a hard-earned habit, which like every other habit, is strengthened by regular exercise. Faith – real, lasting faith – that can "stand up and take it" even on a Cross, must be nourished by daily meditation, by prayer, and the devout perusal of the Scriptures. For listen: strong living is no more possible without prayer and Bible reading than poetry is possible without words, or music without notes!

We are not surprised then to discover that this seventh and last sentence from the Cross is *both a prayer and a quotation from Scripture.* From His youth up our Lord had communed with God in prayer and hidden the Bible in the recesses of His heart. Quite naturally, then, at the last He could reach down into His Scripture-saturated soul and lay hold on God. This is what faith is all about. As the poet sang,

> "Faith is the grasping of Almighty power;
> The hand of Christ and man laid on the arm of
> God; –
> The grand and blessed hour in which things impossible to me
> Become possible, O Lord, to Thee."

Moreover, we all pray in the crises of life. No theory can prevent it. Even Abraham Lincoln, frequently called an agnostic because he hesitated to be identified with the fire and brimstone church of his day, confessed his prayer life saying,

> "I have been driven many times to my knees, by the overwhelming conviction that I had no where else to go. My own wisdom, and that of those about me seemed insufficient for that day."

Yes, in our crises we all pray in one direction or another. Either we cry out to a Fatherly God or we protest against a blind and bitter fate. And either way it is praying. *Prayer is but the outward revelation of the kind of a God we inwardly bank on.* The man who is calm in a crisis is praying to a Father; the man who curses in a crisis is praying to a fiend! But both are praying and banking on their particular kind of a god.

Just now, however, we are not thinking about emergency prayer. We are thinking rather about habitual, daily prayer as

> "the key of the morning's lock and the bolt on evening's door."

Faith is not a dying matter only; it is the everyday surrender of our lives to the voice and will of the Father in heaven.

Most of us find the early morning the best for our daily quiet time. As Henry Vaughn put it,

> "When first thy eyes unveil, give thy soul leave
> To do the like; our bodies but forerun
> The spirit's duty. True hearts spread and heave
> Up to their God, as flowers do to the sun.
> Give Him thy first thoughts then; so shalt thou keep
> Him company all day, and in Him sleep."

It is a proven fact that whatever enters our minds on first waking, perchance a melody or a bit of poetry, will often linger in the consciousness for an hour or more, and may well set the tone for the day. One of the most depressed people who ever came to see his pastor was under treatment by a psychiatrist. When he entered the office of John Sutherland Bonnell, former pastor of the Fifth Avenue Presbyterian Church in New York, he began to pace the floor, wringing his hands and crying. It was impossible to secure his attention even for a moment as he poured forth his woes in an unbroken stream of incoherent talk. When this had gone on for more than a quarter of an hour, Dr. Bonnell was on the point of discontinuing the interview. But instead he began to repeat to the distracted man certain quieting Scripture passages. While his visitor continued to pace the floor in great agitation, the minister said in a quiet but firm voice:

> "The peace of God which passeth all understanding shall guard your mind and heart in Christ Jesus" (Philippians 4:7).
>
> "Peace I leave with you; my peace I give unto you. Let not your heart be troubled, neither let it be afraid" (John 14:27).
>
> "The peace of God is quieting you. The peace of God is relaxing – reassuring – healing you. Peace be unto you. Peace. Peace, Peace, the comforting peace of God."

Little by little the distracted man's agitation began to subside, and after six or seven minutes he sat down quietly. By the time the hour alloted to the interview had ended, he was quiet, relaxed, and cooperative. Before leaving, he was able to smile, even though somewhat faintly. The minister wrote down for him passages of Scripture to read during the day. Most of all he was requested to say over and over at the moment of waking in the morning:

> "This is the day which the Lord hath made;
> We will rejoice and be glad in it" (Psalm 118:24).

In addition the depressed visitor was asked to list for himself on paper each day his blessings – the many things in the past and present for which he should be thankful to God and to others. As the old gospel song puts it,

> "Count your blessings, name them one by one,
> And it will surprise you what the Lord hath done."

Faithfully the man repeated the daily Scriptures and counted his blessings in regular prayer sessions both morning and evening. He continued his use of Scripture and prayer right along with the routine performed by the psychiatrist. After six months his son wrote,

> "Father's condition continues to improve week by week. He looks upon the day he started to quote Scripture and count his blessings in prayer as the turning point in his illness. His faith is stronger now than it has ever been. God certainly has been good to us."

Yes, the fine art of banking on God requires daily Bible reading and prayer.

The other day we ran across a saying of Longfellow's that the Scriptures were

> "writ in the climate of heaven, and in the language spoken by the angels."

At first it seemed to us but a compliment of a literary man who appreciated the Bible's classic prose and poetry. But then we remembered that Mrs. Longfellow had accidentally fallen into an open fire, that Longfellow valiantly but vainly tried to extinguish the flames, and then, when it was all over and Mrs. Longfellow had died, the poet settled down in his wifeless and motherless home to translate Dante to occupy his mind. During this tragic time he wrote,

> "Nothing with God can be accidental."

So, *nothing with God can be accidental* – not even the fatal burning of a loved one! And we knew at once that Longfellow did not come to such a banking trust in God all of a sudden; no, it was the blessed result of his daily devotions with the Book

> "writ in the climate of heaven, and in the language of Him who on the Cross, prayed, 'Father, into thy hands I commend my spirit.'"

III. Finally, consider that not only is our text an evidence of Jesus' daily habit of prayer and Scripture meditation, it is the glorious evidence that, even on the Cross, *he continued to believe about immortality what he taught during his lifetime.* As we have already intimated, the very word used by Jesus in commending His spirit to God implies that He was giving His spirit up but temporarily in the hope of finding it again later on. He was making a deposit of His soul in a safe place, to which, after the crisis of death was over, He would come and recover it.

So faith – banking on God – is not only a power for living here and now; it is also

> "the pencil of the soul that pictures heavenly things."

Or, as another has written,

> "Faith builds a bridge across the gulf of death,
> To break the shock blind nature cannot shun,
> And lands Thought smoothly on the further shore."

Such was the living faith – and the dying faith of Jesus. We, too, must daily bank on God and so make *the safest deposit of all.* And, lo, at the last

> "When our summons comes to join that innumerable caravan where each must take his chamber in the silent halls – we go not like the quarry slave at night, scourged to his dungeon,
> But sustained and soothed by an unfaltering trust, approach our grave

Like one who wraps the drapery of his couch
About him, and lies down to pleasant dreams."

Grant us, O Lord, the quiet confidence of the depositor who entrusts his all into the trustworthy hands that cannot fail. We know that the day draweth nigh when our bodies will be committed unto their final resting places, but we carry on confident that our spirits are always under Thy loving care.

Support us, O Lord, all the day long until the shadows lengthen, and the evening comes, and the busy world is hushed, and the fever of life is over, and our work is done. Then in Thy mercy, grant us a safe lodging, a holy rest, and peace at the last, through Him who is the Prince of Peace. Amen.